I0797844

EVEN IF

I CAN ONLY IMAGINE 2
The Story That Inspired the Motion Picture

EVEN IF

Trusting God Through the Fire

BART MILLARD *(of MercyMe)* & SHANNON MILLARD
with ROBERT NOLAND

DAVID C COOK
transforming lives together

EVEN IF
Published by David C Cook
4050 Lee Vance Drive
Colorado Springs, CO 80918 U.S.A.

A Ministry of Cook Media Global

Integrity Music Limited, a Division of David C Cook
Brighton, East Sussex BN1 2RE, England

DAVID C COOK®, the graphic circle C logo and related marks
are registered trademarks of David C Cook.

All rights reserved. Except for brief excerpts for review purposes,
no part of this book may be reproduced or used in any form
without written permission from the publisher.

The website addresses recommended throughout this book are offered as a resource
to you. These websites are not intended in any way to be or imply an endorsement
on the part of David C Cook, nor do we vouch for their content.

Details in some stories have been changed to protect the identities of the persons involved.

Unless otherwise noted, all Scripture quotations are taken from the Holy Bible, New International Version®, NIV®. Copyright © 1973, 2011 by Biblica, Inc.™ Used by permission of Zondervan. All rights reserved worldwide. www.zondervan.com. The "NIV" and "New International Version" are trademarks registered in the United States Patent and Trademark Office by Biblica, Inc.™ Scripture quotations marked MSG are taken from THE MESSAGE, copyright © 1993, 2018 by Eugene H. Peterson. Used by permission of NavPress, represented by Tyndale House Publishers. All rights reserved; NASB are taken from the (NASB®) New American Standard Bible®, Copyright © 1960, 2020 by The Lockman Foundation. Used by permission. All rights reserved. www.lockman.org; NIRV are taken from the Holy Bible, New International Reader's Version®, NIrV® Copyright © 1995, 2014 by Biblica, Inc.™ Used by permission of Zondervan. www.zondervan.com. The "NIrV" and "New International Reader's Version" are trademarks registered in the United States Patent and Trademark Office by Biblica, Inc.™; NLT are taken from the Holy Bible, New Living Translation, copyright © 1996, 2015 by Tyndale House Foundation. Used by permission of Tyndale House Publishers. The author has added italic or bold to Scripture quotations for emphasis.

Library of Congress Control Number 2025947608
ISBN 978-0-8307-9191-0
eISBN 978-0-8307-9192-7

© 2026 Bart Millard

The Team: Michael Covington, Luke McKinnon, Caroline Cilento,
Judy Gillispie, Brittany Stonestreet, Susan Murdock
Cover Design: Leah Von Fange

Printed in the United States of America
First Edition 2026

1 2 3 4 5 6 7 8 9 10

102825

CONTENTS

A PERSONAL MESSAGE FROM BART AND SHANNON

In March of 2017, MercyMe released our ninth studio album, *Lifer*. The first single to radio was "Even If." Right out of the gate, the song was a huge success and charted faster than anything we'd ever released, including "I Can Only Imagine." "Imagine" was a marathon in gaining popularity, but "Even If" was a sprint. A year later, in March of 2018, *I Can Only Imagine*, the movie, as well as the book, was released. Now, here we are, eight years later—same band, same Bart, new song, new story.

When Shannon and I first told our kids we were involved in a serious discussion with the filmmakers about a *second* movie, right away, they all asked the same question, "What?! What's the sequel?" After I answered, "The story behind 'Even If,'" our daughter Sophie, who was sixteen at the time, came back with a thought I loved as soon as I heard it and have repeated many times to others since then: "Well, I guess for a songwriter, the sequel is just the next song." Sophie's response connected the dots to help me see how both songs, "I Can Only Imagine" and "Even If," along with the real-life stories that led me to write them, were connected in ways I hadn't completely realized myself.

In the 2026 movie *I Can Only Imagine 2*, as well as in these pages, we dive into the details of our lives that began right after the song "Imagine" took off and was heard around the world. As I talked about in the first book, the movie had to portray my story leading up to the song in a run-time of an hour and fifty minutes. With the release of the second film, once again I'm grateful to be given the space to dive deeper in this book and offer much more than the filmmakers are able to do. Producing a movie, every scene costs a great deal of money. Literally, every *second* counts to try to tell the story. Here, while we want every *word* to count, we have the freedom to not only expand but also to explain the details.

The first story was mostly about me and my dad, while this second story focuses on me and my son, our oldest, Sam. In the first book, there were excerpts from my wife, Shannon, but most of the pages dealt with my life leading up to our marriage and the success of "Imagine." In the 2026 film and this book, as in life, she is right beside me from beginning to end, so her voice as my wife and the mother of our five kids is absolutely crucial to the narrative. (Shannon's words are uniquely marked throughout the book, as are Sam's.)

After walking through the many storms of life you are about to hear of, experiencing a devastating domino effect of tragedies, eventually, Shannon and I made the commitment to spend many, many hours in counseling to invest in our lives and future, individually and together as a couple. Because of the amazing healing to which we credit God for leading us to experience, we have no need to walk back through all our painful and vulnerable moments. So our decision to open up and invite you into the living room of our lives is actually not about us or for us. This book is for you. After surviving all the trauma, we believe a part of our purpose on the other side is to share our story to help others find hope in the helplessness and grace in the grief. If you haven't experienced an "Even If" moment in your faith, you will, because, in this life, it's not *if,* but *when*.

Like David, the shepherd turned king who became famous for his conquests on the battlefield for Israel but then came to the end of himself through a series of bad decisions, or Peter, who Jesus called "the rock," yet denied the Lord three times at His worst moments, we follow those who have gone before us in the faith by offering a brutally honest testimony. Our hearts' desire is to present personal evidence of God's goodness amid our humanity, in the middle of our mess.

We invite you to come alongside and walk with us through our story after "Imagine" impacted our lives, as it did so many others. Our hope and prayer is that you are challenged by our confessions in the struggle, that you look inward and be honest about your own questions and doubts, and that you have the opportunity to discover the same truth that, in the end, we did.

> For the LORD is good and his love endures forever;
> his faithfulness continues through all generations.
> (Psalm 100:5)

Introduction

THE GOOD, THE BAD, AND THE BROKEN

When the *I Can Only Imagine* movie and book came out, I assumed that would be all the story that could possibly be told about my life. From my mom leaving my brother and me with an abusive father, Dad's cancer diagnosis and late-in-life radical transformation in Christ, and dealing with his death, to the beginning of MercyMe and then writing our signature song about Heaven—all those events were overwhelming for me to process and release to the world. But I'm grateful for how God has used my song and my story to reach a global audience and change so many lives, which continues to this day.

By the time the credits rolled in the first movie, the Hollywood "happy ending" was achieved and we appeared to have landed in the middle of the pot of gold at the rainbow's end. By 2003, the band's success began to bring industry awards; connections with pro athletes, mainstream artists, and celebrities; sold-out arena shows; and, of course, millions of records sold. Yet, little did we know a very different story was about to be written. When everyone assumed the Millard family's lives had become nothing but blessing, a succession of tragedies came our way. Compounded by the hidden, unresolved trauma of my past, I was brought to a place of brokenness that lasted for years, leaving me to question if or how life would ever be the same again.

I Can Only Imagine 2, the story behind the song "Even If," is all about what began to happen when the first story ended—the year Shannon and I use to mark the timeline of our lives. Creating our own personal BC and AD, we literally divide life into pre-2004 and post-2004 because our journey took a turn we never saw coming. We were blindsided when everything, and I mean *everything*, changed. The first movie and book covered the first half of my life, from childhood to twenty-seven years old. This story covers the second half, from twenty-eight to fifty-two years old, the time of this writing.

Over the years, Shannon and I have seen throughout God's Word that He is up-front and honest with us about this life. Yet in our desperate desire for self-preservation at all costs, we tend to only want to accept the good and the blessed from Him, never the bad and the broken. In Psalm 23, everyone loves the promise of "green pastures" and "quiet waters," but there's no guarantee we won't experience walking "through the valley of the shadow of death" (vv. 2, 4 NASB). When Jesus told us in Matthew 5:45 that "[God] causes his sun to rise on the evil and the good, and sends rain on the righteous and the unrighteous," that wasn't just a warning but a promise. So many believe that when good comes, God is good, but when bad happens, then He must be bad. Or mad. Or we're being punished. But the purpose of faith is to go beyond cause-and-effect and lead us toward trust-and-obey. While most of us go kicking and screaming, we eventually have to make the decision to accept the "rain," "the evil and the good."

In John 16:33, Jesus gave us another promise, "In this world you will have trouble." We can certainly tell you from experience that His words should not be taken lightly. No one should think they have arrived at a place to be the exception to the rule. Yet I'm so grateful Jesus didn't leave us there, when He added, "But take heart! I have overcome the world." Let's just say, after experiencing the "world of trouble," it took quite a while for me to start to discover the "take heart" and "overcome" part.

One thing the past twenty-two years—life after 2004—has shown me: If we are actually going to follow Jesus, then we have to own up to and deal with our doubts as well as our faith, allow for the questions as well as the answers we just thought we knew, and accept the trials along with the triumphs. Which brings me to Job 13:15, a Bible verse you're never going to see on a coffee mug or bumper sticker because we'd prefer to ignore or deny the implication. Yet ten different translations and paraphrases use "even if" to deliver Job's very tough challenge to us in the midst of suffering:

> Even if God kills me, I'll still put my hope in him. (NIRV)

One truth Shannon and I have come to better understand over the years is that when we truly follow Jesus through the dark valleys—through the rain, trouble, and death we experience in this life—in His time, He will lead us to discover how good He is when we are broken.

Chapter 1

THE WHISPERS OF "WHY?" AND "WHAT IF?"

In the thirty-plus-year history of MercyMe, everything changed for us in January of 2002 when "I Can Only Imagine" hit number one on the Christian music charts. As the little ol' worship band from Greenville, Texas, we literally took everyone by surprise, coming out of nowhere in the thriving Contemporary Christian music scene that had experienced a massive amount of acceptance and growth throughout the '90s. Then the real game-changer tipping point came in 2003 when a Dallas mainstream deejay took an on-air dare and played the song as a joke to his listeners. But as the old saying goes, "God had other plans."

The station's phone lines lit up with requests to play "Imagine" again with everyone asking, "Who sings that song?" While there was no such thing yet as "going viral," that's exactly what happened among mainstream adult contemporary radio stations across the US. What a crazy, unpredictable moment when a ballad about Heaven that unapologetically uses the name of Jesus in the lyrics somehow, someway, took off like a rocket, ironically, on a rock station!

The only way this crazy story was able to play out was because God Almighty obviously decided He was going to make it happen.

Our "five minutes of fame" started to get traction, and life for MercyMe began to move us out of our comfort zone. Our previously scheduled shows at Christian events started to mix with requests from promoters and showrunners that are typically reserved only for Top 40 mainstream artists. For example, we would lead worship at a Christian student conference and then be the headliner at a national finals rodeo. We would play at an evangelistic crusade and then be the musical guests on late-night TV like *The Tonight Show with Jay Leno*. The sudden success and demand was absolutely insane.

By 2018, our 2001 album *Almost There*, with the original version of "Imagine," was certified triple platinum, and in 2022 the song itself was certified five-times platinum. Here's some perspective—a record label could spend millions of dollars in promotion and marketing for an artist's single and *never* experience a win like that. In fact, those kinds of losses and misses happen all the time in the music business. A massive hit is a rare exception, especially across so many genres of music. So the only way this crazy story was able to play out was because God Almighty obviously decided He was going to make it happen. There is no other explanation.

Everything was going so well. Exactly the "abundant life" that "good Christians" expect for God to deliver. Then, just as 2004 got started, all hell broke loose. And I don't use that phrase lightly or for shock value. Back in 2018, I knew the story of me and my dad was going to be hard to tell. Now, here I am again and, I'll be honest, this one is definitely harder.

■

Having just celebrated New Year's 2004, I had a rare weekend at home. Typically, following the holidays, there are a few weeks before the music business starts firing on all cylinders and touring begins. On Friday night, January 2, our firstborn, Sam, had been in bed for hours, and then, after I went to bed, Shannon was going to stay up and take care of some of her to-do list in the quiet. Unbeknownst to us, at some point late that evening, Shannon's brother, Chris, had gotten his heart broken. At twenty years old, he was entrenched in the classic battle of becoming an adult and dealing with everyone's expectations of what he was supposed to be doing with his life. At around 1:00 a.m., now the third of the month, he showed up at our house to talk to his big sister.

Chris was a great kid with a solid reputation in town and at his workplace, a very humble job at the Greenville High School cafeteria. But he never saw it as beneath him or thought that he was too good for the work. All the "lunch ladies" there absolutely adored him. He loved on everyone he worked with and served them all. Being a Texas boy, he also owned two horses that he rode and cared for. So Chris was a bit of an anomaly being a cowboy who worked in food service.

Shannon was eight years older than Chris. As a kid, she had prayed for years for a baby brother. So when God answered her countless prayers, she thought he was the best gift ever. With the age difference, Shannon was the ultimate big sister but also like a second mom. Chris was dyslexic, which always makes life so much harder for those who suffer from the learning disorder. If Chris needed help with his homework, Shannon was his go-to. If he got angry at their parents, he went to his big sister. If he blew it with a bad choice, he confessed to Shannon. If he had a flat tire, he called her for help. She may not have always had the answers or been able to handle everything, but that was the kind of relationship they had. Shannon was Chris's on-call rescuer. Because of their close family dynamic, plus me being on the road so much, I didn't get involved or try to intervene when there was an issue. Because of their big sister–little brother connection, they always managed to work things out just fine without me.

After dealing with the details of his heartbreak, Chris and Shannon began to go round and round, talking through his struggles with all the big-picture issues of life. He was begging her for evidence that God is real. She did her very best to offer him answers, saying things like, "Faith is an intangible. You have to decide to trust and believe God. Learn to read His Word and walk in His ways." But Chris had grown up in the same strong Christian home as his big sister, so he already knew all the ready-made answers. He pleaded with Shannon, "Help me figure this out. Show me it's real. Tell me it's worth it." Chris was longing for an experience, like most of us do, which, of course, no one can make happen for someone else. With all those burdens and questions on top of his fresh heartbreak, for the first time possibly ever, Shannon was running out of answers for her brother.

Shannon

Around 1:30 a.m., I realized I needed help, told Chris to wait, and walked down the hall to our bedroom to wake Bart. After rousing him from sleep, I said, "Hey, I need you. I've never dealt with something like this with Chris. I'm desperate for your help." Trying to wake up and process what I was asking, understandably, Bart was hesitant at first. Over the years, I had asked for his assistance with everyday, normal things with my brother that were beyond my ability, but never something this heightened or this heavy.

While waiting for Bart to answer, I suddenly realized Chris had come down the hall and was standing at the bedroom door. In his upset state of mind, he interpreted Bart's delayed response as not caring, which, of course, wasn't true. As I turned around, Chris said, "He's not going to come, is he?" Hearing my brother's question, I looked back at Bart with a now-there's-no-choice expression on my face. With that, Bart got up, and we all went back to the living room for round two.

Now, as both of us were engaged with Chris in this emotionally driven back-and-forth, he would be a bit aggressive and disrespectful to Shannon one minute and then get convicted and start crying the next. While we knew he was a Christian, we could see Chris was struggling with what so many young people do at that age: being ready to own your own faith but trying to figure out how and what that looks like, to no longer just blindly follow the God of your parents and family but find your own belief. That's a tough battle for anyone to resolve. The proof of his struggle came when, at one point, Chris confessed, "Man, I just want to get right with Jesus."

The conversation went on for hours as Shannon and I listened patiently, trying everything and saying anything we could think of to help him. That was definitely one of those times when you're silently praying for wisdom to know what to do but starting to doubt if you're making any headway at all. You start to feel like you're caught in a vicious cycle. Somewhere around 3:00 a.m., my physical, mental, and emotional exhaustion got the best of me. I finally reached the point Shannon did earlier when she had come to get me. I ran out of options just like she had. Now, we'd both hit the wall. In frustration, I stated, "Chris, somebody just needs to take you out back and knock some sense into you!"

Of course, I didn't mean that literally. Shannon had been responding to him as his big sister, and I was acting like his big brother, which was exactly my relationship with Chris. Exhausted and frustrated himself, he shot back at me, "Oh, okay! Are you going to be the one to do it?!" Seeing and hearing his response, I softened immediately and reassured him, "No, no, I'm just messing with you, Chris. You really need to get some sleep. It's been a long night. You'll have a better perspective tomorrow."

Unlike what he'd done many times before, Chris ignored my advice to stay and go to sleep and, instead, quietly got up off the couch and headed for the front door. Just as he opened it, he stopped and, looking back at both of us, somberly said, "Tell Sam I love him."

By now, it was somewhere between 3:00 and 4:00 a.m. on January 3. As the door closed and we saw the lights of Chris's truck shine through the window, we both thought something about his goodbye didn't feel right. Only a few minutes had passed when Shannon said, "Bart, that was weird. You need to go find him and bring him back here."

Shannon

Within seconds of my brother making that statement and heading out the door, I felt a sudden sense of urgency. Whether he consciously realized it or not, my brother sounded like he was saying goodbye. There was a strange finality to his words. Chris was not one to leave things undone, and this was certainly not resolved. The state I was in was very much unlike me. I froze. I could not move. I didn't jump off the couch and run after him. Confused by my own hesitation, I thought, *What's wrong with me? Get up! Go!*

The internal battle in my heart was that I had just invited my husband into a difficult situation with my brother for the first time, and it had gone badly. Bart had stood up for me, so I felt the tension of honoring my husband and letting go versus getting up and going after my brother. My compromise was to ask Bart to get in the car and find Chris.

Knowing it was best for Shannon to stay with Sam, I grabbed my shoes and keys and headed out. By that point, I didn't know where Chris was going, and depending on how fast he was driving, I knew he had a decent head start on me. I went anywhere I thought he might have gone. Initially, we had made the assumption he might have been drinking before he got to our house, which turned out not to be the case, but I knew if he had, he would never have gone back to his parents' house. Most likely, he would have driven to a friend's.

Hours later, as the sun came up over the horizon, I had struck out. No Chris. Anywhere. Especially back then, Greenville was not that big. With nowhere else to look, I got back home around 7:30 a.m. Absolutely drained from being up all night and the emotional toll, I went to bed.

A short time later, Shannon's dad called her. Someone had driven up on a one-car accident and called 911. After being awake all night and emotionally exhausted, Chris must have fallen asleep at the wheel, run off the road, and, at the point of impact, been thrown from the truck. The final detail that made his tragic death even harder was that the road he was on was one of the routes back to our house. The only one I hadn't driven. Because Shannon was Chris's hero, if he had any sort of disagreement with her or felt bad about how he left, his pattern was always to come back, apologize face to face, and resolve any issue. He was clearly returning to set things right with us.

Obviously, a moment we would have given anything to have experienced.

The sudden, unexpected news from her dad absolutely devastated Shannon.

Shannon

The rest of Saturday, which spilled over into Sunday, was spent meeting with police and authorities to answer questions in between sobbing and feeling such deep, unspeakable grief. Of course, all our extended family and huge circle of friends were coming by, so those days were a blur. To pour salt in the wound, Sunday, January 4, was Sam's second birthday and a big family celebration had been planned for that evening. But instead of getting ready for a birthday party for our son, we were at the funeral home making final arrangements for my brother. Because Sam was still just a toddler, he didn't know any different. But with him being my first child, I got very angry with God and the horrible questions of "Why?" began. I kept asking, "Why did You allow this to happen to Chris?! Why did You let this happen right before our son's birthday?! Why would You allow what should be such a fun, sweet day to be turned into a horrible tragedy?!"

Talking with one of my closest friends, she said, "Shannon, I know Chris dying right before Sam's birthday feels horribly unfair right now, but in time, this will actually turn out to be a blessing. Every year, celebrating Sam's life is going to lift you up out of the memories of grief and sadness. There will always be joy on the other side of that day."

In the moment, all I could feel was anger at her for saying that to me. I wasn't in any shape to process a sentiment like that. I thought, *Never! That is never going to happen*. But just as she said, down the road, I realized my friend was right. What appeared to be cruel at the time would prove to be redeeming in the years to come.

Along with the shock of being woken up to hear what happened to Chris, an internal accusation showed up right away that punched me in the gut so hard that I felt like all the breath had been knocked out of me. Because of my past, I was wired to feel that I was responsible for *anything* bad that happened around me. Even in situations that were totally out of my control, my mind would find a way to justify how I had somehow caused the crisis or that the problem was me. A condemning voice would whisper in my ear, "Well, you screwed up again, didn't you, Millard?" My response was to quickly agree that somehow I had, always guilty as charged.

That's when I began to replay the last words I said to my brother-in-law: "Somebody ought to take you out back and knock some sense into you." And then his angry response started screaming in my head, "Oh, are you going to be the one to do it?!" With that scene playing on repeat in my mind, I took it a step further: *That's why he left our house and went driving around.* Like a defendant standing before the judge of my own conscience, I dropped the gavel and declared, "I must be responsible for Chris's death! It's just a matter of time before the authorities piece all this together and come for me! Do I need to go ahead and turn myself in?"

While this is so hard to admit and I know it can sound really paranoid, for any of us, the state of shock and grief at the news of a loved one's sudden, tragic death does strange things to our minds and hearts. Irrational? Yes. Unfounded? Sure. But understandable? Certainly. Because God originally made His creation for the Garden, He never intended for us to have to deal with this sort of trauma. All the toxic feelings we can experience amid crises only proves that truth.

Regardless of anyone's reassurance, I couldn't shake the unbearable weight of guilt and the overwhelming sense of shame. I grabbed hold of this new accusation and made room for it among all the emotional baggage from my childhood and teen years. Before, I always found a way to stuff it down and press on like I was fine. But what made this time different was death. While I had struggled with my dad's passing, I never felt responsible for his cancer. But a twenty-year-old who was like a little brother to me when my voice was possibly the last one he heard? To me, this was very different.

Shannon said she was battling the "whys," while my constant "what ifs" began attacking and torturing my thoughts.

And the one person I couldn't run away from was me.

Shannon

I became a Christian at six years old. I've never known life apart from Jesus. In fact, I struggled a bit in high school when I began to hear other people's testimonies of "I was in the pit, hit bottom, and then I found Christ." I remember thinking, *Oh, I've always known Jesus. Maybe that's a bad thing?* This question led to doubts, such as, *I don't have a story like that, so do I really know Him?* I wrestled for a couple of years with wishing I had that kind of tale to tell, which is crazy when I look back. Of course, I eventually reached a point of realizing I hadn't missed anything, except maybe a lot of heartache. In time, I became very grateful for my story.

Our life in Greenville, Texas, was surrounded by parents, siblings, grandparents, uncles, aunts, and cousins. As Bart's career began to take off, I was so thankful that I could see God's obvious fingerprints in the timing of His blessing from MercyMe's success and our own family growing with Sam's birth. Often, I thought, *How could life possibly get any better? Everything is exactly the way it's supposed to be.* I had my family and Bart's family, a good church and great friends. We all loved Jesus. We were doing Bible studies together and taking our kids to Mothers of Preschoolers. My life was what I had always hoped and dreamed it would be. Even still, I was a little nervous about Bart getting so busy because of the band's popularity, asking obvious internal questions like, *How are we going to balance all this? What's ahead? What is our life going to look like?*

The day Chris died, my little utopia was shattered. My previously untested faith was shaken. On January 3, 2004, I stood face to face with the kind of trial I never anticipated would come.

Chris and I were raised in a strong Christian home, and our family was in church every time the doors were open with my parents constantly serving in ministry. While we never questioned their love for us and they were always our biggest cheerleaders, the generational dynamic was present in them not showing very much physical affection. In short, no one in our family was a hugger.

That early morning, when Chris first walked in the door of our home, before all the questions and deep discussion began, he collapsed on our couch, sobbing. I was surprised by the fact that I had never seen him show that level of emotion. Letting go and crying that hard was very unusual for him. As I watched and wondered what to do next, as clear as I have ever sensed the Lord's voice speaking to me, in my spirit, I heard, "Hold him tight." Because offering that sort of physical gesture was not at all the norm for us, immediately, the battle in my head started as I questioned, *Really, God? Should I do that? Isn't that going to be weird?*

Taking a deep breath with an okay-here-goes attitude, I got up, went over to the couch, sat down as close as I could to Chris, and wrapped my arms around him. Obeying the words I heard, I "held him tight." His response? My little brother melted into my arms, laid his head down in my lap, and sobbed so hard that my pajamas were soon soaked with his tears.

Today, thinking about how I went against my natural instinct and our family dynamic, I'm so grateful, so thankful, because that moment and memory is now one of the greatest treasures of my life. I had the privilege of being the last person on this earth to hold my brother before, just a couple hours later, he would be held tight in the arms of Jesus.

For our Chris ...

No more heartache.
No more questions.
No more tears.
No more pain.

He will wipe every tear from their eyes, and there will be no more death or sorrow or crying or pain. All these things are gone forever. (Revelation 21:4 NLT)

Movie Moment

THE STORYLINE

When Andy Erwin and the Kingdom Story team began to walk through the scenes they had shot for the movie, they had to make some very tough calls. Oftentimes, at this point in filmmaking, entire scenes and even actors' performances have to be cut to arrive at telling the best story in the allotted runtime and to make the movie as compelling as possible for the audience.

For *I Can Only Imagine 2*, because of the nature of our entire story during this season, the decision was made to keep the storyline focused on the theme of relationships between fathers and sons, a solution I fully supported. That meant Chris's death, and other events you will read about in these pages, would not be in the film. As the team began to work through early edits, they did some test screenings with small audiences. I was told that several people asked, "Did all that *really* happen to them?" When I was told those reactions, I laughed and said, "Yes! And that's not even the entire story!"

At the end of John's Gospel, he wrote some very intriguing words: "Jesus performed many other signs in the presence of his disciples, which are not recorded in this book" (20:30). Basically, the four Gospel writers had to each divinely choose what to include in their accounts of Jesus. John tells us in this verse that quite a few people and situations (for our purposes, some "scenes and actors") had to be cut. As for our story, the film followed that biblically inspired principle. But that's what I love about being able to also write a companion book—we get to tell you everything.

And, yes, "all this really happened."

Chapter 2

HOW LONG COULD THIS LAST?

After Amy Grant first heard "I Can Only Imagine," I agreed to let her record it on her next album. Being such a huge fan of hers, I was honored that Amy wanted my song. In an amazing turn of events, she made the selfless decision to give "Imagine" back, telling me she believed the song was intended to be sung only out of my personal experience. She felt like MercyMe should be the artists to release it to the world. Needless to say, that offer and advice from her forever changed our lives. From that, the friendship we forged also led to her very generously and graciously agreeing to go out on the road with us on that tour to open the show each night. (In case you're wondering, no, her gesture was not lost on me, and yes, being on tour with her was very humbling and surreal.)

In February of 2004, a month after Chris's funeral, we were two weeks into the "I Can Only Imagine" tour. One night after Amy's set, I was walking down the venue hallway toward the stage when my phone rang. Seeing the number of a close family member, I knew I needed to answer. I was told the devastating news that my Uncle Rick, who was my absolute hero and one of my top-five favorite people on the planet, had died suddenly from a brain aneurysm. Just as I was starting to sense some relief from being consumed by grief the past several weeks, the news of another tragic death felt like being thrown back into the fire.

In shock again, I immediately threw my phone down the hall as hard as I could. My only thought was to put as much distance as possible between me and the thing that had delivered more terrible news. For the next five minutes, I fell apart, lost it, sobbed. On my knees with my head in my hands, the pain in my heart was excruciating. But I knew a large crowd was literally waiting on the band to go out. The old saying "The show must go on" is a very real expectation for those of us who make our living performing for people who pay good money to buy a seat to see us. Regardless of our troubles, the job description is to help people forget about theirs for a couple hours. Somehow, I managed to pull myself together, wipe away the tears, shove the grief down in my chest on top of all the other pain, and pray my emotions would stay at bay. With a forced smile, I walked out to the mic at center stage to sing about the hope that I was just barely hanging on to myself.

Just as I was starting to sense some relief from being consumed by grief the past several weeks, the news of another tragic death felt like being thrown back into the fire.

Shannon

Two weeks after Chris's death, we were finally able to celebrate Sam's second birthday with family and friends. Then Uncle Rick died a month to the day after we buried my brother. Bart had just gotten back out on the road when we received the call. So here we were again, reeling from the unexpected death of a close family member. Like I said, we have always been a *very* tight family, so by now, I was in serious denial, solely for the sake of my own survival. I wasn't refuting that my loved ones had died, but I was in a battle from the onslaught of questions surrounding Chris's death and how those were affecting my own spiritual struggle. I constantly asked myself, *What do I believe now? Do I still feel like God is with us?... With me?*

Yet taking care of our two-year-old son while Bart was on tour, I didn't have much time or emotional bandwidth to look up or look inward for very long. Meanwhile, every single day, I was trying to be there for my parents, who had lost their other child. My daily pep talk to myself became "Just take care of your baby, pretend like you're strong and happy, and be a support to your grieving parents."

Two months later, in April 2004, Shannon and I got the incredible news that we were pregnant with our second child. Finally, something good had come our way; some sunshine had cut through the storm clouds. Thank God that summer and fall were mostly uneventful. We were working hard to find normal again, or at least some sort of new normal. Somehow, we managed to hold ourselves together and press on with life. Shannon's due date was December 10, so our year-end had been planned completely around that time. But in early November, at the start of her thirty-fifth week of pregnancy, our next major life event showed up unannounced.

Shannon began having serious contractions, to the point that we knew we needed to go to the hospital. When the first nurse realized how premature she was and began to monitor the baby, she made a comment out loud that should have been kept to herself: "Oh, this is bad." My wife, with no hesitation, asked for the charge nurse on duty. When she came in, Shannon requested the woman leave our room and be taken off our care. Her exact words: "Find someone who can be more encouraging, please." Within a few minutes, asked and answered, a new nurse walked in with a totally positive attitude, which we very much appreciated.

As with any preemie, there were all the initial concerns that can cause a lot of questions and fear. But on November 4, 2004, our daughter Gracie Ryan was born six weeks premature with absolutely no complications or issues. (Ryan was Chris's middle name.) They didn't have to admit her into the NICU. She didn't even need oxygen. Even though she weighed only five pounds, Gracie was perfectly healthy. After three days in the hospital, just for absolute certainty she was okay, we were so grateful that both mom and daughter were released to go home.

Because of MercyMe's demanding schedule and Shannon's and my ongoing struggle with grief and sadness, we were way behind in getting life at home ready for our new baby. In the hospital, we realized we didn't have anything, not even a car seat to get Gracie home. Her room at the house was finished and ready, but that was all. Shannon is very detailed, a list maker, and a planner. My wife is never caught unprepared, so this was definitely a rarity for her. We started asking family and friends to help us gather what we needed for our first little girl. For Shannon and me, this surprise was a wake-up call to the reality of where we both were emotionally and just how much the year had affected us.

■

The 2004 American Music Awards were to be held on November 14 at the Shrine Auditorium in Los Angeles with MercyMe nominated for Favorite Contemporary Inspirational Artist. With the original due date, that trip had looked perfectly fine on the band calendar, but Gracie's premature arrival had changed everything. After talking it over, Shannon told me that because everything was good with our newborn daughter and she had plenty of family around to help with Sam, she was fine for me to go on with the band as scheduled.

Besides being nominated for an award, we were asked to be presenters as well. As the six of us waited backstage, someone with the production team began explaining to us that at the last minute they decided to bump the Christian category from being televised. Their decision was no surprise to us; we were accustomed to those kinds of calls being made about our genre. But we were still going out to present the Favorite Adult Contemporary Artist award. Sheryl Crow, Harry Connick Jr., and Norah Jones were the nominees. They also wanted us to read the teleprompter with the legal jargon for how the "votes are tabulated," a spot typically relegated to some accountant. Then, nonchalantly, the guy added, "Oh, and by the way, you won the Inspirational Artist award." We were informed we would be handed our trophy unceremoniously backstage later. (In case you're wondering, the other nominees that year were Steven Curtis Chapman and Third Day.)

Regardless of being punted off the broadcast, we had won, so we were all laughing and high-fiving each other. Without warning, we heard the announcer say, “Now, please welcome MercyMe!” We walked out on the stage under the bright lights in front of the TV cameras sporting suspiciously huge grins on our faces to a crowd of “who’s who” in the music industry. No one had a clue we had just won our category’s award. After Barry and I traded off reading our lines from the teleprompter, I opened the envelope and announced the winner, Sheryl Crow. When the show was over, with the time difference between Texas and California, I knew it was too late to call Shannon. I decided to wait and reach out the next morning before we got on the plane to give her the good news that we had won. A rare perk in a tough year.

■

Early the next day, sitting at the gate at LAX, I called. When Shannon answered, I said, excited, “You’re not going to believe this, but we won … we actually won!”

Sounding distracted, she responded, “That’s awesome.... As soon as you get home, we’re going to need to take Sam to the hospital.”

Surprised and confused, I asked, “Hospital? What’s wrong?”

“Well, after you left, Sam started having some symptoms that concerned us, so I went to the pediatrician and they did blood work. They think he may have diabetes.”

Knowing little to nothing about the disease, I responded, “Okay, yeah, sure. I’ll be home as quick as I can after our flight lands.” Hanging up, assuming diabetes was something you get over, I thought, *All right, so we’ll have to make sure Sam lays off sugar. Maybe loses some weight. How long could this last?*

Shannon

With Bart leaving to go to LA, my mom, Claudette, a.k.a. Grandmama, who had been coming over every day to help me with Gracie, spent the night. She was doing laundry, cleaning, cooking meals, serving any way she could, and, of course, wrangling Sam. Ever since he was a baby and, at that point, almost three, he had always been a joyful, sweet child. We hadn't really dealt with the "terrible twos" you often hear about. But Mom and I began to notice he was getting uncharacteristically aggressive. To keep him from getting out of his bed at night and roaming the house, we had placed a baby gate at his door. That night, he got angry and bull-rushed the gate, doing his best to knock it down, something he had never tried. He had also thrown his toys at a large window in our living room. Clearly, between the gate at night and the window during the day, the theme was trying to break out. With a brand-new baby sister in the house who was getting a lot of attention, we all knew it's not unusual for an older sibling to have to adjust to the sudden change. I made the safe assumption that he was acting out because of Gracie's arrival.

The next morning, my mom requested that everyone at the house come into the kitchen. My dad was there, along with Bart's mom, Dell, a.k.a. Nana. I could tell something was on Mom's mind that was very serious. She opened the refrigerator and grabbed an almost-empty gallon of milk, then said, "See this? I just bought it yesterday. Did any of you drink some?" She looked around and expected everyone to answer, as if someone were in big trouble. But we all said no, which turned out to be exactly what she suspected.

Next, Mom pointed over at Sam, who was playing nearby, and said, "That baby drank a gallon of milk in a day. A day!" Putting two and two together, she realized that, as different family members had come in and out of the kitchen, Sam would ask for a glass of milk. And who isn't okay to give a kid a glass of milk? So everyone had, not knowing anyone else did. Then she added, "Also, he wet the bed last night, not just a little, but soaked the sheets two different times, to the point they had to be changed."

In no uncertain terms, Mom declared, "Something is not right."

As I had been doing for quite awhile after the deaths in our family, I immediately denied there might be a problem and calmly protested, "No, Mom, nothing is wrong. Sam is just acting out because of his new sister. That also explains why he wet the bed. This will pass."

Mom took hold of both my arms, looked me square in the eye, and stated, "Shannon, I think Sam has diabetes. You have to call the doctor."

While I knew my mom had a lot of life experience, in that moment I didn't give her enough credit to think she could diagnose my child. Still stuck in my grief, I got so mad, feeling like this was some sort of accusation. That's when I exploded. "My brother died! We lost Uncle Rick! I have a preemie baby! And now you want to tell me there's more?! ... How dare you! Don't say that to me! And I don't even know exactly what diabetes is."

Mom looked at me, as only a godly, loving mother and grandmother can, and repeated with intention, "Shannon, you need to call the doctor."

Our pediatrician was a family friend. We had gone to the same church for years. His daughter had been close with Chris. One of the many things I love about life in a small town is the tight community. I answered, "Fine, Mom. If you'll leave me alone, I'll call him."

On the phone, after explaining to the nurse what was going on with Sam, she told me to bring him in right away. Because our doctor knew us all so well, he understood how badly we were struggling from such a terrible year. After hearing the concerns and his examination of Sam, he was very gentle with me, being careful not to let on how dire the situation could be. Much like my mom had spoken to me so deliberately, the doctor stated, "Shannon, I need you to take Sam to the hospital right now and get blood work done. I'll send them what I need, and, as soon as I get the results, I'll call you."

Still in denial that this could be something serious, I agreed and did as he asked. First thing the next morning, not long before Bart reached out from LA, the doctor called to say, "Shannon, pack a bag. You need to take Sam and go to the children's hospital in Dallas right away."

Confused, I explained that Bart would be flying back in a few hours and I wanted to wait on him. He hesitantly agreed, but made it clear that we had to go as soon as Bart arrived.

Even after hearing the doctor's clear directive, I was thinking, *What could possibly be this serious?*

Arriving home from the airport, I found Shannon's parents and my mom there to take care of Gracie. We strapped Sam into his car seat and made the hour drive from Greenville to Children's Medical Center in Dallas. To put life in perspective, on the way there, like some empty water bottle or discarded french fry container, my American Music Award was lying on the passenger floorboard, completely ignored. Ironically, much like the TV producers had decided to cut us from the broadcast to focus on the more famous artists, now we were also pushing the accolade aside to prioritize Sam.

By this point, all I actually knew was that Sam had been oddly aggressive, started sweating profusely, had an insatiable thirst, and constantly had to go to the bathroom. I was also told he had gotten into some candy left over from Halloween, so I figured his blood sugar may have skyrocketed from a few too many pieces. Like Shannon, I had no idea what the urgency was all about.

In ICU, we were informed that Sam's blood sugar was 847 and that a normal two- to three-year-old child's number should be in the 80 to 100 range. While of course we knew the difference between 100 and 800, we had no real reference as to what the escalation actually meant. The entire time, the doctors and nurses were clearly working in emergency mode. Now we were the ones trying to get answers to our questions as they immediately started injecting Sam with insulin in an attempt to get his blood sugar down. For a toddler, they said they had to introduce the medication at a very slow pace to make sure there would be no adverse reactions or complications.

Minute by minute, we were starting to get the picture that Sam's condition was indeed serious.

Finally, one of the doctors gave the diagnosis, confirming that our almost-three-year-old son had type 1 diabetes. News that would impact us all for the rest of our lives, but no one more than Sam.

■

As Shannon and I sat beside his bed in ICU the rest of the day and into the night, we also noticed the activity going on with another family next to us whose child was evidently going through the exact same thing. Eventually, we picked up on the fact that his blood sugar was higher than Sam's. The doctors and nurses appeared to be even more concerned and tense with their situation.

At that time, over two decades ago, being diagnosed with type 1 meant spending a week in the hospital for them to teach us everything we needed to know to manage the disease. They showed us how to take a syringe, draw the insulin from the bottle into the tube, and then, using an orange, coached us through the correct way to give Sam a shot. The amount of information, including the complicated process we had to learn of regularly pricking his finger and checking his blood, was incredibly overwhelming. And, remember, all this happened suddenly. We had no warning or lead-up to this moment. Because of all we had gone through thus far in 2004, I was in denial and struggling with the thought of Sam's condition actually being permanent. The term *chronic* just wasn't sinking in.

Finally, one of his nurses took my arm and pulled me away from everyone. She squared up with me, looked me in the eye, and, like a drill sergeant dressing down a private, stated, "Mr. Millard, you need to pay attention. This insulin that I'm showing you how to administer to your son is life support for him ... from now on."

I will never forget that moment of her verbal slap-in-the-face, you'd-better-wake-up warning. Now, with my eyes wide and fully tuned in with her, she continued, "Type 1 diabetes does *not* go away. Your son is not going to get over this. His pancreas is dying, or has already died, and his body can no longer make its own insulin. I'm showing you how to give him what he will need to survive."

As soon as my come-to-Jesus meeting with the nurse ended, I was so overwhelmed that I told Shannon I had to go to the car to grab something. But that was just an excuse to catch my breath and escape the tension for a few minutes. When I got to the elevator, the couple whose child had also been in ICU was there waiting for the doors to open. I immediately noticed the look on their faces and that they were holding a teddy bear and a few kid's items. And then I looked down and saw it ... an empty stroller. That's when the terrible reality hit me. They had just lost their child.

As I stood there in shock waiting for the elevator, the dad looked over and recognized me from being next to them all day. In a somber tone, but trying to encourage, he said, "Hey, hang in there, okay?"

I made eye contact and nodded, but as soon as the doors opened, I acted like I had left something in the room and told them to go on. Walking around the corner into an empty hallway, I fell apart. The realization that their child had come in the same day with type 1 diabetes, was in the room next to us, and now they were going home without him was beyond what I could handle. And we found out later that Sam's blood sugar level was only 200 lower than their child's.

The "somehow this is my fault" accusation kicked in again. In my emotion, the thought that swept over me was, as Sam's dad, my job is to take care of him and "fix" anything that breaks. *Anything.* Even though the nurse had just told me, "You cannot fix this. You can't fix your kid." The harsh reality of her words and the sight of that couple going home without their son caused me to feel the heat of the flames once again.

Shannon

Once I finally wrapped my head around Sam's condition, my fighter response kicked in. My instinctive attitude said, "We're going to do this, so buckle up and get ready!" As a Christ follower, ultimately, my biggest motivation is that Satan will not win. We are not going to allow the darkness to overtake us. I want to climb into the ring and punch the enemy in the face. For years, I have constantly made that declaration to our kids.

The week we spent in the hospital with Sam was one of the hardest times of our lives. Our pediatrician told us later, "I was so afraid and praying for you because I thought you only had a day or so before Sam would be gone." That's how close we were to another tragedy in this terrifying year. Yet we were incredibly grateful for the miracle that God had allowed us to realize what was going on and get Sam to the hospital in time to literally save his life.

In Matthew 6:34, Jesus said, "So don't worry about tomorrow, for tomorrow will bring its own worries. Today's trouble is enough for today" (NLT). Seeing that to be true, now more than ever, I had a feeling life was going to be lived one day at a time.

Chapter 3

GRACE IN THE GRIEF

While we were still in the hospital going through diabetes parent training, the weekend was fast approaching. MercyMe was scheduled to go back to California to the Rose Bowl Stadium to play at a Billy Graham Crusade. The band's manager, Scott Brickell, a.k.a. Brickell, called to check on us. He knew we also needed to make a decision whether to cancel or go. Of course, being invited to do anything for Billy Graham was an incredible honor. With the travel arrangements made months before and no word from me yet, the rest of the band was getting ready to fly out as planned. Once again, "the show must go on," so everyone assumed we were leaving, especially because of the nature of this event.

The decision of staying versus going was weighing heavy on me. With that, here comes another confession: At this point in the band's career, I had kept these feelings to myself, but I was beginning to resent the burden of being the only one who had to make or break a show. If one of the other guys had an emergency or something important planned with family, we could hire a substitute guitar or bass player or drummer. While our core fans would notice, they'd still come and have a great time. The music and background vocals get covered in a way that no one would be able to tell a big difference. But subbing in another lead singer and front man? That's another story entirely. Fans are attached to the voice they hear in your songs and on the radio. Then, especially for a Christian band, there's the added importance of what you share between songs at a live event.

Trust me, I'm not making a direct comparison to me and MercyMe, but how many people would go see U2 if Bono wasn't going to be there or The Rolling Stones if Jagger couldn't make it? Bands like the Eagles and Fleetwood Mac became exceptions over the years because they literally have several lead singers and most of the hits have not been sung by just one person. Worst-case scenario, they have to cut a song or two at a show. But the band dynamic is just different when there's *one* lead singer and front man. For that reason, I have always chosen to go at all costs. I carried that responsibility without complaints or excuses. Plus, that burden also fell perfectly in line with the "everything is my fault" guilt complex if I ever did decide to cancel.

After giving Brickell the company line of "I'll go. Shannon and I will figure out a plan with our family here at the hospital," I finally broke down and admitted, "I can't leave Sam. I can't leave Shannon. I can't go." Of course, he understood. In fact, everyone understood my not going under the circumstances. Reassuring me, Brickell said he would make some calls and let me know the outcome. Before long, he called back. Dr. Graham's team had given an interesting counteroffer. They wanted to send a private jet to pick me up in Dallas around 1:00 p.m., fly me to LA, drive me to the stadium, where Dr. Graham would meet with the band, pray for Sam and our family, and then fly me back that night, all at their expense. I would be gone from the hospital for a matter of hours, not overnight. Sitting in Sam's room with several extended family members, after Shannon heard their offer, she said, "Bart, we respect Reverend Graham so much, and it's a huge honor. You need to go."

Because I had never been on a private jet before and I was a bit dazed by this whirlwind decision, I asked my brother, my cousin, and my uncle who were at the hospital, "Hey, y'all want to fly to California, get an In-N-Out burger, and go meet Billy Graham at the Rose Bowl?" (Sounds like the ultimate Christian fever dream, doesn't it?) Like the Texas redneck family that we are, with their best deer-in-the-headlights expressions, all three responded, "For real? Seriously? Yeah!"

With the four of us sprawled out in the spacious jet seats for the three-hour flight, we landed in LA right on schedule. The Graham team picked us up with a police escort. I loved being able to give my family members this one-of-a-kind, once-in-a-lifetime VIP experience. When we pulled into the back entrance to the stadium, we saw thousands of people lined up outside the gates. After meeting up with the guys in the band who had arrived earlier, one of the team members led us to a large tent set up on one side of the stadium. Dr. Graham's security team looked like the Secret Service. We had never seen anything like it.

On the other side of the stadium, we saw an identical tent to the one where we were brought, also enclosed so you couldn't see inside. They were the same, except over on that side were a couple hundred people gathered around, clearly a lot of news media with microphones and cameras. Quite a contrast to our side, which was completely empty except for my family and the band. Assuming Dr. Graham was over there with the crowd, I was starting to wonder if someone had made a mistake and we had been escorted to the wrong side. As the minutes passed, my concern was that the event was going to start and we might miss our opportunity to meet him. And that was the only reason I had agreed to leave my family.

Just as my fear peaked, Dr. Graham walked into our tent unannounced, accompanied by one lone security guard. Having obviously heard me express my last concern that we were on the wrong side, he smiled and said, "I don't normally agree with not telling the right hand what the left hand is doing, but this time I made an exception." He had somehow created a diversion so he could have a few minutes alone with us before going over to make his appearance at the media tent.

After everyone was introduced, in his classic, warm, pastoral demeanor, Dr. Graham hugged me. Then he gently placed his hand on the back of my neck, looked at me intently, and like the spiritual father that he was to so many, said, "I'm so sorry to hear about Sam." Then, he asked, "Do you mind if I pray for him?" Unable to speak, I simply nodded. As he began to intercede, every time he said Sam's name, he was very intentional, so deeply personal, as if he wasn't just praying for someone's son, but for his friend, like he had known us our entire lives. Every time Dr. Graham said, "Sam," more tears came. We had only met minutes before, but the way he voiced his care and concern was deeply authentic. The moment was so personal that it's hard to describe. But here's the part I will never, ever forget and that will be with me for the rest of my life: Dr. Graham prayed, "Please, Father, either heal Sam or … allow Sam to change the world as a diabetic."

He said "Amen" and then told me, "Bart, thank you for coming and letting me pray for your family." It's impossible to convey how humbling that moment was for me. As he said goodbye and walked out of the tent, one of his team came over to me and stated, "Thank you for coming. You can leave for the airport whenever you're ready. That's all Dr. Graham wanted to ask of you." I responded the only way I felt was right: "Well, since we're all here and the band is set up, the least we could do is go out and sing 'Imagine' for the crowd." So, just before Dr. Graham went to the podium to preach the Gospel, MercyMe sang about Heaven. Afterward, we decided to stay to hear his message and see the altar call. At the end, we were escorted out of the stadium, driven back to the jet, and flown home to Dallas. (Oh, and yes, as promised to my family, the limo driver stopped by In-N-Out Burger before we got to the airport.)

That was one of the wildest experiences I ever had in all my years with MercyMe.

A moment only God could have orchestrated.

■

But with just over a month left on the calendar, 2004 wasn't finished wreaking havoc on the Millard family yet. At the beginning of December, doctors discovered that my father-in-law, Frank, had a grapefruit-sized tumor in his head. Immediate surgery was required to try to save his life. They told all of us in the family that, while their hope was for the removal to be a success, they were only giving him a 40 percent chance of survival. I have no idea how doctors come up with their numbers, but saying only four of ten people make it through this type of surgery was terrifying for us all.

With this news, I got angry and began questioning God again: "Are you kidding me?! We're a couple weeks from Christmas in the worst year of my life and now this happens!" In moments like that, I often think about David, the greatest songwriter in history, and the way he was always so bluntly honest with God, like in Psalm 13:1–2:

> How long, LORD? Will you forget me forever?
> How long will you hide your face from me?

> How long must I wrestle with my thoughts
> and day after day have sorrow in my heart?
> How long will my enemy triumph over me?

Then, through my gritted teeth and tears, I calmed down and presented my plea. "God, I can't lose this guy now. My dad is gone. Chris is gone. Uncle Rick is gone. Frank is the cornerstone of this whole family. Please!" To make matters worse, the doctor encouraged us all to "say our goodbyes" in case Frank didn't make it. I hope you never have to go through that. What makes it so tough, especially for the Christian, is you want to have faith and hope to believe the Lord is going to pull your loved one through, but you also know plenty of good, godly people don't make it. Happens every day. So you have to balance faith with reality and treat this moment like it could be the last.

Shannon

I have always been a daddy's girl, so hearing from the doctors that he might not survive pushed me way past my breaking point. January 2004 brought my brother's death, and now this horrible year looked like it would end with my father dying. Would my mom and I really be alone with just the two of us left in our family? Trying to filter all this trauma through my faith brought about some interesting "aha moments" for me.

First, I realized how much we as Christians throw Scripture around, too easily misquoting or misusing the Word. At the absolute worst times, well-meaning people will quote verses like Romans 8:28 to you: "God causes all things to work together for good" (NASB). Is that true? Yes. But timing and context are very important when we quote the Word to help others and be sure we don't unintentionally hurt them instead. Who wants to hear in that moment the implication that a loved one dying is "God causing good"?

Or someone may say, "I know God will give you the peace that passes understanding." In the middle of such grief, is His peace available? Of course. But in the moment, what I didn't understand had nothing to do with peace but the confusion of why this had to happen at all. This wasn't about our peace but God's purpose. I vowed when I was given the opportunity in the future to comfort someone, I would be much more careful to remember how I felt when I was in the pit of despair. I wanted to remember what I *didn't* need to hear. There's a big difference between speaking sympathy and expressing empathy. That's why one of the best choices is to just be present with someone who's hurting. Just be there in the moment and be okay with the silence.

The other thing I realized was how we can flippantly use some saying that a lot of people assume is Scripture when it's not. Here's one: "God won't give you more than you can handle." Do you think when Job had lost all his children and everything he owned, and was sitting on the ground in pain from sores all over his body, that he would agree with that bumper sticker slogan? I seriously doubt it. And there are plenty more examples in the Bible. The truth is that God in His sovereignty will most certainly allow us to experience more than we can handle. He will bring us to the end of ourselves so we can see what He is capable of and what we aren't. Maybe that saying came out of a misunderstanding of 1 Corinthians 10:13: "And God is faithful; he will not let you be tempted beyond what you can bear." Enduring to escape temptation is not the same as enduring a life-altering trial.

Dad's doctors were telling us that the outcome on the other side of the surgery, should he survive, would most likely leave him blind or mute. None of those options were "good." None of those brought "peace." Regardless of whether they could successfully remove the tumor, they were telling us he was going to come out very different and would no longer be the dad I knew and deeply loved.

After I told him what I feared would be my final goodbye, I will never forget lying down on that nasty hospital floor in his room to stay close to him. By that point, I had totally checked out of life. I had nothing left. If I wasn't crying, I was sleeping, all from depression. Broken, this was officially too much for me to take. As I've said, by nature, I am a fighter. I'll put on the gloves and start swinging. But that entire year, aside from Gracie's birth, had only been bad outcomes, so why should I believe my dad was going to escape being the next one in our family to die?

When they came to take Dad to surgery, I told Bart I couldn't be there when the doctor came out. I told him I would stay in the hospital room and he could wait to hear whatever news was given. So Bart and my mom kept watch, waiting outside the surgery-room door.

I lost all track of time, but I will never forget the moment Bart walked into the room where I was laying. He bent down and gently said, "Shannon, your dad is good. They got it. He's fine. He came out perfect." Dad was not only in the four out of ten to survive but the minority that comes out as good as before. When all you have known is bad news, getting good news like that feels very surreal. It's hard to process. You wonder if you're dreaming. You struggle to believe that what you're hearing is actually true.

My mom had gained so much medical knowledge that she could have been made an honorary nurse. The proof was her seeing the signs of diabetes in Sam. And this wasn't the first time my family had dealt with Dad being diagnosed with a brain tumor. When I was ten years old, we almost lost him. From everything Mom learned that first time around, when Dad began showing some slight signs and symptoms, she was able to pick up that something was off. She was the one who insisted that they go to the doctor, which led to them discovering his second brain tumor. Mom's insight and discernment definitely had a hand in saving Sam's and Dad's lives.

God will bring us to the end of ourselves so we can see what He is capable of and what we aren't.

Praise God, Frank came out the other side completely fine. The surgeon was able to remove all of the tumor. The procedure and his recovery could not have gone better, and the heart-wrenching goodbyes were not necessary after all.

Let me rewind a bit, back to Chris's death, to tell you one of the many reasons my father-in-law meant so much to me. At the family visitation before the funeral, Frank came over to me, placed his hands on my shoulders, looked me straight in the eye, and stated, "Bart, this is not ... your ... fault." We literally fell together, holding each other up in as tight of an embrace as I have ever had as the tears took over our words. Frank knew that I desperately needed to hear the patriarch of the family tell me I was not responsible for the death of his son, my wife's brother, Sam's uncle, and my brother-in-law. This man that I love and respect so much was able to help me at least begin the process of healing from my accusations and self-condemnation.

So let's recap, shall we?

Right after MercyMe and I had our dreams come true with a massive hit song ...

My brother-in-law, Chris, was tragically killed.

My beloved Uncle Rick died of a brain aneurysm.

My daughter Gracie was born six weeks premature.

My son Sam was diagnosed with incurable type 1 diabetes.

My father-in-law, Frank, had a brain tumor, and we had to tell him goodbye in anticipation of his death.

A few weeks later as our family celebrated Christmas, we were so grateful to have survived with our last trauma of 2004 turning out to be good news. But Shannon and I were so exhausted—emotionally, mentally, and spiritually spent in every way.

Even after going through Dad's passing, and then Chris's and Rick's sudden deaths, still nothing was more trying and intense than Sam's diabetes. At the time, I had no capacity to articulate the feelings of being a father who's been told your kid has an illness that has no cure. A 24-7-365 burden of that magnitude wears on you more than the grief of death. When someone dies, there's a point where you begin to see that the absence will heal over time. But something like a chronic disease with no promise of healing has an overwhelming everyday presence. Being a parent in a circumstance like that brings seasons of stress and worry that are devastating and debilitating. For so long, my inability to process it all was matched only by my deep denial.

When you keep getting burned by the fires of life, particularly over a relatively short period of time, you become conditioned to the trauma. As you begin to get over one crisis, you start to not just dread the next one but expect it. Impending doom starts to override your sense of peace. When I was a kid, after my dad had done things like break a dinner plate over my head or raise his fist to threaten me, any time he would make a sudden movement, I would flinch out of a trained reaction. I realized, while it had been many years since I experienced that, now I was flinching at life.

Saying goodbye to 2004, I was very concerned what the next year would bring. More fires? More pain? More heartache? Or would God finally start to turn things around, allowing the trials and tests to let up, just like He did with the story of Job that Shannon referred to, where healing, restoration, and blessing eventually come?

I knew that the success and demand of the band, coupled with all these tragedies and crises, had deeply affected me.

As I fought this strange mix of pain and numbness, my faith was struggling.

I was broken.

Shannon

Psalm 139 has always been a very special chapter of the Bible for Bart and me. God had used it as a confirmation for how we knew we were going to get married one day. We had been separately praying about marriage, and the Lord showed us each the words of that chapter. When one of us brought it up and the other said,

"Wait, He told me that too," we were amazed. After my brother died, I was led back to that passage, specifically verse 16: "Your eyes saw my unformed body; all the days ordained for me were written in your book before one of them came to be." In short, even before we are conceived, God knows our birthday and the day we die.

Our humanity wants to think we can control things. At least, I know that's what I like to try to do. All the tragedies of 2004, including the trauma of Gracie's premature birth and my dad's brain tumor, created a crisis of belief for me. I was battling the enemy's lies and my own struggle of what I was going to choose to live and believe. Taking in Psalm 139:16, I began to see death from a different perspective. If those words are really true, then my brother was going to die that night, no matter what. If I would have chased him down before he drove away, whether he stayed at our house and slept there or left like he did, God had ordained the number of Chris's days.

Being honest, I had to wrestle with that verse for a while. But I finally came to the conclusion that I can't pick one truth out of the Bible and say, "Oh, I 100 percent believe that," and then on a different truth say, "Yeah, I don't know about that one." The Bible is all or nothing. It's not a menu we choose from but the meal we are served. In fact, a lot of people today tend to separate out only what they want to believe to attempt to keep their lives nice and comfortable. But that's not what following Christ is about. In Luke 9:23, Jesus told the crowd, "If any of you wants to be my follower, you must give up your own way, take up your cross daily, and follow me" (NLT). That's not a safe, soft, feel-good invitation. There's going to be some suffering and dying to our own will.

Here's some evidence of the level of God's sovereignty I began to understand: Two weeks after we brought Gracie home healthy was when Sam's diabetes was discovered. If she had been born around her due date, we would have literally been in the aftermath of trying to learn how to care for Sam. Had my mom not been there helping us care for our newborn, we might not have realized what was going on with him soon enough to save his life. Gracie's original due date was December 10. My dad's surgery was on December 10. Yes, "all the days ordained for me were written in your book before one of them came to be."

As I began connecting all those dots, I started realizing, through all the pain and heartache, the Lord's hand was indeed on us and His timing is never early or late, but just right. His presence *was* with us through it all. At that point, I decided to choose to believe every day that this God we trust in is very real. *My* God. My faith was my own. No one would be able to talk me out of holding on to His truth in my heart.

Chapter 4

THE FLOWER CHAIR

In the Gospels, we read story after story that gives various situations and locations where people experienced Jesus. What was often just as fascinating as what Jesus did was how the person responded afterward. Some, like the rich young ruler or the religious leaders, ended up walking away without believing or even deciding to oppose Him. However, many not only chose to accept and follow but left behind the very thing that most represented their lives at the moment their faith connected to Jesus' invitation.

For Peter and Andrew, they left their fishing boat.

For Matthew, the tax collector's booth.

For the woman at the well, her water jar.

For Zacchaeus, his money.

For Mary Magdalene, her demons.

For Bartimaeus, his beggar's cloak.

For Bart, the flower chair.

Yes, I know I'm not in the Bible, and no, my name is not short for Bartimaeus, but if you thought to yourself just now, *One of these things is not like the others*, well, you'd be wrong. Let me explain. For me, the flower chair in the corner of our living room became just as important a marker of a significant transformation in Christ as Peter's fishing boat or the Samaritan woman's water jar. All these tangible and seemingly insignificant things became deeply personal representations of the life left behind after surrendering to Jesus.

Maybe you have your own "flower chair," something that will forever serve as your memorial or reminder of what Jesus has done in your life. If so, it doesn't matter if it makes sense to anyone else, does it? A marker might coincide with what led to salvation, but maybe not. It may simply connect with some moment when a very real revelation came that brought radical change. There are a lot of people who would say they came to faith in Christ as a child or teenager, but then some life circumstance, or in my case, multiple circumstances, brought them to a place of desperation and deep need, which eventually led to a renewed understanding of who Jesus is and what He wants to accomplish in our lives.

■

Heading into 2005, MercyMe's success brought about more offers to play than there were days in the year. While Brickell was fielding the calls from our booking agency and vetting everything based on the particulars from the promoters, my go-to answer became yes. You may ask, "Now, wait a minute, Bart. You just told us how much you were struggling, right?" Yes. But because of that state, my goal was to do any- and everything I could to try to escape the debilitating pain I was experiencing in the aftermath.

Out on tour, I had the built-in "luxury" afforded to me under the guise of "I have to leave home to go out and make a living." To sing in Cincinnati, I have to go to Cincinnati.

My job requires me to be away, which, in that season, allowed my overwhelming reality at home to be "out of sight, out of mind." Life on tour is a very copy-and-paste existence with a controlled schedule, making it easy to pretend all the trauma back at the house doesn't exist. (To pull back the curtain on so many touring artists and musicians, Christian or not, this is actually a very real problem in being able to create a sort of virtual reality on the road, often bringing major stress on marriages and parenting, too often ending in broken homes and distant relationships.)

Grief and depression aside, there was a round-the-clock stress in dealing with Sam's diabetes. Of course, the problem was not our son, but the literal 24-7 management of his disease. Six to eight times a day, we had to give him a shot. If you've never had to deal with something like this, and I hope you never do, let that sink in for a second: We had to give a three-year-old a shot six to eight times a day. And when I say "we," what I mean is one of us had to hold him tight to keep him from fighting us while the other gave him the shot. For a toddler, there's no such thing as reasoning with him. To his little mind and heart, every few hours, Mom and Dad were intentionally hurting him by either pricking his finger to draw blood or placing a needle in him. And when Sam would tell us he wanted something to eat, we had to calculate what we gave him or sometimes tell him no, depending on his carb count and numbers for that hour.

I could see why it would be hard for a child to understand that you love him when you keep hurting him, while your only goal is to keep him alive. One of the toughest aspects as a parent is you are forced to push past your feelings of compassion, guilt, and helplessness or you're not going to make it. For that reason alone, Shannon and I were both exhausted and emotionally checked out. Then when I was gone to work half the month or more, she had to deal with the shots by herself or have a family member or friend help her. Slowly, over time, when I was home, I wasn't present and engaged.

Now that I've given you the setup, let me introduce you to the flower chair ...

■

We had this old, bold floral-print piece of furniture in the corner of our living room. When I got home off the road, I would collapse into that stupid chair for hours on end, totally vegging out. I couldn't seem to face life. Reality was too hard. So sitting there, whether staring at the TV, a laptop, or into space, I just wanted to let life pass by without anyone noticing I wasn't taking part.

When the kids wanted me to play with them and I didn't want to leave the chair, they would start climbing all over me, like I was some kind of human jungle gym. Sometimes, I would make up games we could play that wouldn't require me to get up. With them being so young, I was able to fool them into thinking we were actually playing together. As soon as we would finish one made-up game, they would excitedly call out, "What do you want to do next, Daddy?" They didn't seem to be able to tell the difference between gathering around the flower chair and being in the backyard. Mission accomplished. There were also times when I ignored them and paid no attention. That is, unless they accidently knocked the laptop out of my hands or got between me and the TV.

That first year, after all the deaths in our family, because I had gotten to know so many pastors over the years, we were offered a lot of advice. One of those nuggets was "Everyone grieves at a different pace," meaning, as a married couple, we weren't likely going to match up on where we were in the five stages of grief—denial, anger, bargaining, depression, and acceptance. One person might get through a stage in a few weeks, while another takes months. This is one of those human dynamics where "it takes as long as it takes." No one can rush grief. Pushing just makes everything harder. You can't will or fool yourself into thinking otherwise.

Divorce can happen when, for example, a couple doesn't realize or acknowledge that one spouse is still in the anger stage while the other one has moved into depression. Anger is often aggressive, while depression can appear passive. One spouse can begin to feel like the other is cold and heartless when, in fact, the grief has just changed stages. As for me, I was obviously internalizing everything but just didn't understand what was happening or how to deal with my feelings.

Once, when Shannon and I were in the middle of an argument, I stopped, turned, and walked away, completely shutting down. Out of desperation and deep frustration, she said, "Yeah, go ahead, go sit in your flower chair and pretend we're not here." Surprised, I asked, "*What* are you talking about?"

That's how little attention I had been paying to what I was doing. I never even realized my default parking spot was the flower chair. To be completely transparent about that season in our life, Shannon had every right to leave me, and a lot of women would have. But thank God, she didn't. My wife was amazingly patient with me. The incredible truth is that, the entire time, she was struggling just as much as I was, yet she somehow managed to show me so much grace. Probably too much grace.

Shannon

I knew Bart was saying yes to most of the band's offers to go on the road. Over time, I could see that his mindset became *If I'm going to have to be at home, then I'll just sit here. Somehow life feels better in this chair*. (A bit of a different spin on the ad where Nicole Kidman is sitting in an AMC Theatres seat, saying, "Somehow, heartbreak feels good in a place like this.") I would ask him questions like "Why are you in the flower chair? Did you notice you've been there all day? Do you want to get up and engage with us?" That chair became this inanimate character in our house that represented Bart's emotional state. The irony was the fabric was emblazoned with very bright, bold, colorful flowers. Hence, the name we came to call it.

The entire time Bart was in the chair, I felt the same as he did. But I *couldn't* sit in the chair. I had to attend to the growing number of little people running around our house, even though I had very little to give them beyond meeting their physical needs every day, especially with everything it took to stay on top of Sam's diabetes. My own toxic feelings, which just manifested differently than Bart's, were another reason I didn't have anything left to give anyone. On the surface, I put on an act of being upbeat to keep life in the Millard household going, but inside, I was absolutely hollow. My smile wasn't real, just a mask hiding the intense pain.

As Bart mentioned, so many couples in this circumstance end up in divorce, because the grief and hopelessness eventually drive a wedge they can't find a way to overcome. Then bitterness and resentment take root, and the separation begins. The wife gets cynical because the husband is checked out and not helping. The husband develops a grudge because all he hears is his wife nagging him. This is also why anyone in these circumstances is ripe for an affair. Meeting someone who isn't in the middle of your mess and who appears to be normal and happy and shows any positive attention at all can easily create a temptation.

Yet often, I kept circling back to the question I knew Bart was struggling with: "Was Chris's death my fault?" Even though he didn't voice those feelings of guilt very much, part of me was holding on to empathy for Bart. Every once in a while he would let something slip, and I would think, *Oh, there it is. The blame and guilt are still there.* That realization gave me grace for him because I knew that was a bigger struggle than the one I battled. I was sad that I lost my brother, while Bart was holding on to a sense of responsibility for his death, which sits in a very different place. While I didn't believe anything was actually Bart's fault, I also had no idea how to help him get past his constant accusation of himself.

I remember seeing a statistic at the time that said for a couple who lost a child, the divorce rate was 80 percent. Bart and I were watching the damage that grief was creating in my parents' marriage after losing Chris. We could see the battle of their individual pain and emotions. I recall telling them in one particularly volatile moment, "Now, hold on. You're both still grieving, but grieving *very* differently. That doesn't make either one of you bad or wrong. You're just in different lanes on the same road. You have to somehow find empathy and grace for each other."

Navigating their struggle helped Bart and me be cautious of letting ours get too far or too deep. Where my parents were being very vocal about their struggles, we tended to keep quiet about ours. But there were times when we would confess to each other, "We don't want to do what they're doing. We have babies to raise, and we know we love each other. Let's keep trying our best to fight this."

The only thing we knew to do was show up every day to whatever extent we could.

In being the lead singer and front man of a band for twenty-plus years, as well as the primary voice to field all the many questions from both mainstream and Christian media interviews, I have found there is one singer who has set the standard for sharing his full humanity, his most vulnerable thoughts, and his life of faith, both onstage and off. Agree with him or not on any issue, U2's Bono has invited the world into his innermost thoughts on a regular basis for decades. One of his quotes that challenges me is "Honesty, vulnerability and a good amount of courageous faith allows you to cry out in your bewilderment and not lose your belief in the process. These things allow you to wrestle your faith rather than lose it."[1] Shannon and I certainly didn't feel very courageous, but we were working hard to not lose our belief. We were trying to wrestle with our faith so we wouldn't walk away.

For the rest of this chapter, I'm going to veer away from the story a bit to share some of what I was battling during the flower-chair season and also one of the dynamics that drew me to be out on the road. While your circumstances will likely be different, my prayer is you'll be able to connect these thoughts to your own pain and struggle. I want what I share to encourage you to be honest with yourself about your own circumstances. If you're in a great place right now, consider depositing this in your bank because, likely, not too far down the road, you're going to need to make some withdrawals on these same topics.

■

One of the most common things I have heard people say about me is how I've always been able to be extremely vulnerable when I share onstage between songs, as if the audience and I are in the middle of a deep yet obviously one-sided conversation. Somehow standing up there, I can bare my soul. That is, as long as there's distance between the stage and the front row. And, honestly there are a lot of nights when I can't see anything out there in the blackness except, ironically, the glowing neon red of the exit signs.

I've been told many times, "Man, I couldn't do what you do. How can you share your feelings in front of ten thousand people like that?" What they don't understand is that's the safest place to share your heart—thirty yards from people who can't talk back. Behind the mic, I'm in control of what I say and how much I say with no fear of interaction or contradiction. Yet when someone who is not in my immediate circle tries to engage with me, I struggle to talk about my life or open up, because one-on-one doesn't feel safe to me.

I think the best way for anyone today to understand this dynamic is to look at social media. You don't even have to have an account to see that people will post things for the world to read that they would never say to anyone's face or use their real name to back up their statement. Getting bold or outspoken when you can't see anyone isn't an expression of bravery as much as cowardice. We see that play out online many times every day. Social media has given anyone and everyone a "microphone" to speak to a faceless crowd. As for me, I get invited to speak under the spotlight into the dark each night.

A very similar experience to being onstage for me is being behind the wheel of a car. With my severe ADHD, there's something about being in the driver's seat, looking out at the road ahead, that keeps my thoughts focused. I think that's why I have written more songs while driving than sitting in any room, because I can accurately fixate on my ideas and feelings. Driving and onstage, complete focus is crucial or you crash and burn. (Case in point, you never want to shout, "Thank you, Dallas," when you're in Houston. That makes it almost impossible to get the audience back.) On many nights in some arena in the US, I have actually processed a thought for the first time right in front of a crowd. Believe it or not, when they heard it was also the first time I heard it. While sharing, I'll discover or uncover something powerful for me in the moment, and the tears that people see glistening on my face in the spotlight are very, very real.

James 5:16 tells us, "Confess your sins to each other and pray for each other so that you may be healed." That's incredible counsel from Jesus' brother, because everyone has issues and questions that we need to speak out loud to escape our isolation that sin has created. The second we voice a confession or thought, it can no longer roll around in secrecy in our heads and hearts but becomes real. That's when, like James said, healing can begin. I suppose in some strange way, while the audience may see me like a pastor sharing truth with them, the better analogy might be that the stage is like my confessional booth and the people are the priests, listening intently while I confess.

It should be no surprise to you by now when I say that I hold my emotions and feelings close most of the time. As Shannon said about her family earlier, the Millards certainly weren't huggers either. I didn't grow up expressing affection and have never been able to fully make the transition. But I believe that's also a big part of why I can express my feelings in such a way that causes people to relate to my songs. My greatest outlet to speak what I need to say comes through writing lyrics that can impact others by giving them the words for their own feelings, doubts, and struggles.

■

Through these challenging years, I have also come to see that the role of being a father and the expectations that come with it are difficult for men to open up and be vulnerable about. As dads, I'm sure we all wrestle with the responsibilities, particularly when something bad happens in our families. I want to address the kind of feelings we can have when things happen that are out of our control.

Good dads have a "not on my watch" attitude. That's exactly why, when a crisis occurs, it's easy for men to feel like they failed. On the other side of 2004, that was the mindset I had. That's also the way I was raised. With everything that had happened to my family, I felt like I was in a lose-lose situation. The obstacles in front of me seemed insurmountable. Growing up, the toxic worldview I inherited from my dad told me that if something went wrong, severe punishment was next. That's why I made the connection that everything bad that happened was on me. When all the horrible events of 2004 went down on my watch, I felt not only that I had messed up but that I was to blame. My failure as a husband and father brought the hammer down on me.

To give you an example of how severe this was in my life, if our family made plans to do something outside and it rained, all I could think of was how I should have scheduled the outing on a day when it was sunny. After leaving the Chick-fil-A drive-through, if Shannon asked, "Where's my coffee?" whether I had accidently left it off the order or the "my pleasure" kids messed up, I had failed as a human being.

Rationalizing my responsibility for the little things meant any major life event that went wrong just upped the stakes. For example, feeling like I had killed my wife's brother. Or Sam's diabetes was somehow on me. Or Gracie coming six weeks early was due to stress I had caused Shannon. Because of constant failure, I gave myself a life sentence in the flower chair. But as I sat there, all I could think about was how not being able to get out of the chair was just more failure. I was caught in a vortex of guilt and shame. Being home was an ever-present reminder of my failure, to the point that when we returned from the road, I would take the long way to the house. I firmly believe that, on some level, so many husbands and fathers feel this way but are never going to voice those confessions. For many men, their workaholic overtime at the office is their version of me staying out on the road.

The first song I wrote to acknowledge these struggles was on the 2006 *Coming Up to Breathe* record with the 2007 single "Bring the Rain." My process of prayer was "God, this is so hard, but if, for some reason, this is what I have to go through, if this makes me closer to You, then bring the rain." Let's revisit David's Psalm 13 to add verses 5 and 6:

> But I trust in your unfailing love;
> my heart rejoices in your salvation.
> I will sing the LORD's praise,
> for he has been good to me.

■

Over the last decade or so, a trendy buzzword or phrase has been used a lot—"impostor syndrome," meaning, rational or not, you feel like a fake. Post-2004, as a well-known Christian artist, I struggled with constant guilt that I was trying to fool everybody. I knew that playing the part of a super-Christian onstage was easy. You can start to feel like the Holy Spirit is in a road case like a guitar or drum kit. You unload His case, get Him out for everyone to see, then pack Him back up until the next show. Anyone can fake the role of "strong Christian" for an hour in front of people who can't reach you or talk back.

This dynamic is true for a lot of pastors as well, because most of their congregations see them onstage for only half an hour or so on Sunday mornings. The danger is you can actually convince yourself that you have it all together, making you feel bulletproof onstage. That is exactly why, every few years, a scandal breaks in Christian music or at a megachurch involving someone who has been singing or preaching about Jesus, but the headlines report he has been living like the devil.

My fear of God was colliding with my own feelings that He knew I was a fake. I've heard pastors confess that the topics they preach the hardest on are often the very issues they struggle with the most. During this season, my battle was putting my family first. So, onstage, I would say things like "If you're Jesus on the road, then you should be Jesus at home." That was me preaching to myself. At the same time, I had a fear that people could see right through me. I figured they knew I was an impostor. While I never told an audience I thought I was an incredible dad, I would say things I knew I needed to hear when no one else was telling me the truth. (To be clear, everything I sang and shared on any night was the same truth I sing and share today. God was God then and He is God today, working through sinners like me.)

Starting in 2005, there were too many years when I was just going to work, clocking in, and working my shift to make a living. I was struggling with being home, but I wasn't enjoying being on the road either. I guess it's the old truth that if you're miserable, you take miserable with you wherever you go. I began to ask myself, *How much longer can I do this?* But I knew everyone on our team was relying on me to show up and sing so they could pay their bills too. The horrible irony here is I was at my most unhealthy spiritual place at the height of our career. Our most successful season was the hardest time of my life.

When I expressed my anger at God, my prayer would usually consist of just one word: "Why?" As a husband, as a father, as an artist, as a man, I was in way over my head.

And I knew it.

God was God then and He is God today, working through sinners like me.

My way-too-long season in the flower chair brought conflict to everything at home. My depression was causing me to suddenly snap over the smallest, stupidest things. I've never been physically violent, but I developed a short fuse and would get extremely frustrated in seconds. For example, when we got up to the speaker at a fast-food drive-through, if everyone wasn't ready to give me their order, I would snap. I never knew what simple thing might set me off. Those unpredictable moments were really hard for Shannon and the kids. When I would get angry, she would get upset with me for how I acted, as well she should.

Another huge frustration for Shannon was when, in the middle of the night, we had to check Sam's blood sugar. I either wouldn't wake up to help or pretended I was asleep, forcing her to have to do it all. She understandably had some moments when she would tell me, "Look, I shouldn't have to do this alone when you're home." She was already carrying the full load when I was on the road, but then I would come home, go to the chair, and do nothing. We had so many blow-up moments from her asking, "Hey, can you please give Sam a shot? I'm in the middle of something." I would be so zoned out that I would give the injection wrong or not mix the contents correctly.

Sam's doctor was continually tweaking the dosage because of his blood sugar levels. I would avoid helping for so long that the regimen would have changed and I wasn't up to speed. Not realizing, I would measure the amount from two weeks before. Shannon kept a whiteboard with all of Sam's current information clearly written out. Naturally, she would ask me, "Did you look at what's on the board?" Many times, she would just say, "Never mind, I'll do it myself."

There were a few times of me being checked out that put my son's life in danger. One time, I wasn't paying attention and gave him too large of a dose. On the drive to urgent care, I was thinking, *Oh my gosh, I killed my son.* The fear and guilt were overwhelming. I'm sure for Shannon, I was like having another child around. Thankfully, by God's grace, during that season even in the emergencies, Sam was okay.

Before, I told you that after 2004, my *faith* was hanging by a thread, but now, I was ignoring and denying the fact that, while I was in the flower chair, my *family* was hanging by a thread.

Chapter 5

BACTERIA, BACKDRAFT, AND BREAKUPS

Over the next several years, Shannon had to navigate me in the flower chair and everything that came with that dysfunction. Along with Sam's care, pregnancies, births, and babies, looking back with twenty-twenty hindsight, I can see that she was crying out for help. I can see it now, but I couldn't then.

But with Shannon's I-can-do-this spirit, most people just didn't understand everything she was having to deal with. Even though family and friends were always available and very helpful, as a woman, wife, and mom, she wasn't allowed the time she needed to grieve. She didn't have the opportunity to stop and deal with her own pain.

Shannon

After Chris died, I felt the reality of suddenly becoming an only child. Even as an adult, I would never wish that role and burden on anyone. With my one brother now gone and Bart having one brother, we both knew all too well what life in a small family was like. While we never had some sit-down, map-it-out discussion, especially with just one sibling left between us, Bart and I both knew we wanted a large family, if the Lord would allow. For the big families we knew with a lot of siblings, when they became adults, they appeared to have a better chance of remaining close. Even with our dysfunction, we decided to go with a "the more, the merrier" mindset. We imagined how awesome Christmas and other holidays would be with a bunch of us gathered together. That scenario just felt right to us. While neither of us really knew what we were doing, we were in agreement we wanted our family to grow over the next several years. So here's the result ...

Our second son, Charlie, was born on March 29, 2006.

By early 2008, I got pregnant again and, on December 11, 2008, our second daughter, Sophie, was born. When we had her, now outnumbered two to one, we still had the feeling we weren't done. Someone wasn't here yet.

In midsummer of 2010, we found out I was pregnant. On March 21, 2011, our third son, Miles, was born. After we had him, we were absolutely certain that this was the family God had called us to have. At that point, Bart and I agreed that the Millard family was complete. If you've lost count, we have five children—two girls and three boys—oldest to youngest, nine years apart.

For the first two kids, Bart named Sam and I named Gracie. When we had Charlie, we asked Sam what he thought his brother should be called. The movie *Charlie and the Chocolate Factory* had just come out, so you can guess Sam's answer. For our last child, Charlie and Sam both decided on Miles because of Miles Austin, the Dallas Cowboys receiver. The middle names are all family, but the first names were a group effort, as long as we all agreed. One thing is for sure: We look at our family now and say, "Life would not be right if even *one* of these kids wasn't here."

■

Even though having a large family was a mutual decision, for Bart, I felt like the pressure of providing for a growing family just intensified his commitment to the flower chair when he was home off the road. On the other side of that coin, our need for provision offered even more reason for him to say yes to more shows, which, of course, meant being gone.

Navigating Sam's diabetes began to offer our marriage a strange blessing, giving Bart and me a constant focal point to keep us connected and having to communicate, whether he was at home or on the road. Away, he would call from whatever city he was in and, after checking on us all, we would settle into our usual focus as Bart would ask, "How's Sam? How are his numbers?" The common denominator of fighting together for our son's life kept us grounded. Like they say, "What doesn't kill you makes you stronger," and we were certainly not dead yet. But just as we were feeling like we might be getting our feet up under us to stand, stop crawling, and try to walk, another fire swept in.

But this one came with a mystery that required some due diligence.

I began having some dental issues and went in to get it checked out. To this day, I never offer to anyone what I do for a living, but at a doctor's office, I always forget that my insurance card says, "MercyMe Incorporated." If they've heard of the band, they know what I do. After an exam and X-rays, the dentist informed me I had some vertical fractures from unknowingly grinding my teeth and clenching my jaw. While I'd had no idea that had been happening, I really wasn't surprised that any stress-related physical symptoms would show up.

The dentist went on to explain the procedure they would have to do to repair the damage. That's when he suggested an interesting proposal: "We can fix your teeth, but if you have ever given any consideration to getting veneers, this would be the perfect time." I had always hated my smile, so the possibility was definitely tempting. But when they came back with the quote for all the work, I experienced sticker shock. Because the veneers were considered cosmetic or a vanity procedure, our insurance wouldn't touch it. I told them I would need to think about what to do, but likely would only agree to whatever our insurance would cover.

After I got home, the dental office called and a lady asked, "Hey, are you in the band MercyMe?" I answered, "Yes, how did you know?" She responded with what I had forgotten: "We saw it on your insurance card. We know who you are." That's when they made me an offer I couldn't refuse. "If you'll agree to do some endorsement ads and a commercial where we can use your name and pictures of your new smile, we'll do the entire procedure for free." Wondering if there was a catch, I repeated the info, and she affirmed the offer was real. I remember second-guessing and asking Shannon, "Is it weird that I'm enhancing my looks, like Botox or a facelift or something?" Let's just say I quickly got over my reservations and agreed to the deal.

No surprise that the band was in the middle of a tour, so trying to schedule the four required visits proved to be difficult. That's when they gave me an alternative to accommodate my limited availability: Do everything in one marathon day, around ten hours of nonstop extensive work. We set the date and I managed to survive, coming home with a completely new set of pearly whites, as promised. One long, tough session with my mouth held open wide for way too long. But I was done.

Shannon

I remember well when Bart came home and told me the dentist's plan to cram four sessions into one long day. I heard him out and then said, "Um, that really doesn't sound very wise. Are you sure?" But with Bart's vocation being one where he's photographed and videoed constantly, for the dental enhancement to go beyond the repairs from the stress damage made a lot of sense. When he came home late that afternoon from the appointment, his teeth looked amazing, so I had to reconsider that I may have been wrong. His already-contagious smile was now incredible.

About a week or two later, I woke up one morning and literally could not get out of bed. I felt like I went to sleep in my thirties and woke up a ninety-year-old. Some kind of weird Rip Van Winkle experience. I looked the same, my smile was awesome, but I struggled to move. Shannon had to help me with everything, even getting dressed and putting my shoes on. That first day, I wondered, *What in the world is wrong with me?!*

Shannon

When Bart woke up that morning with the very strange symptoms of his body going stiff and his joints swelling and in pain, he was like an elderly man. I've always been an investigator when something goes wrong, so I went into my normal research mode. Looking online and reaching out to the folks in my circles, I asked questions of anyone I thought might have some knowledge of his symptoms. Going through Bart's recent history of where he had been and what he had been doing, the one anomaly turned out to be the marathon day of hyper-speed dental work.

When I went to see a doctor, she asked, "Have you done anything out of the ordinary in the recent past?" My answer was no, because I was thinking more along the lines of *Did I fall or hit my head somewhere?* At some point, the doctor looked at the paperwork I had filled out prior to the visit. One of the common questions was "Have you had any surgery or procedure done in the past year?" The only thing I had written in that blank was my dentist appointment.

She told me, "I missed this the first time through, but tell me about the dental work." When I explained what they had done, she immediately knew what happened. "When they filed your teeth down, your gums were completely exposed for hours. Obviously, bacteria got into those vulnerable areas and into your bloodstream, and now your immune system is attacking every single joint in your body, trying to fight off the infection."

Shannon

In my mission of trying to talk to anyone who might be connected to a dentist, when I asked, "If somebody did that procedure in a single day, could it hurt you in any way?" the majority took a protective stance and said no, assuring me it was fine. But then one dental hygienist's honest answer confirmed my suspicions when she said, "Absolutely, if they don't clean your mouth thoroughly, then start digging in your gums and doing that much work throughout your entire mouth, any remaining bacteria, even from their gloves, can get into your bloodstream and cause an infection."

The mystery was solved when the doctor gave Bart's debilitating illness a diagnosis: reactive arthritis. (Ever heard of it? Neither had we.) Arthritis? Of course. Reactive? No. Much like how, when we first heard the term *diabetes*, we had no idea about the serious implications of type 1. Keep in mind Bart's symptoms as you read the Mayo Clinic's definition: "Joint pain and swelling triggered by an infection in another part of the body.... This condition usually targets the knees, ankles and feet.... Reactive arthritis isn't common. For most people, signs and symptoms come and go, eventually disappearing within 12 months."[1]

The definition perfectly described what Bart was experiencing. The eye roll came for us at the "isn't common" part. *Of course!* But the knockout punch was seeing twelve months. *A year?!* Suddenly, we were facing yet another difficult season. Bart just wanted his teeth to look better, which they most definitely did, but now he was so sick he *couldn't* get out of the flower chair! I had to help him get dressed and help him bathe. Once again, we were back at "for better or worse, in sickness and in health."

While I suffered through the reactive arthritis symptoms, we never canceled a show. Someone would help me up any stairs or ramps, but once I walked out to the mic, I was good. From day one, I have mostly stood in one place on the stage anyway. I never move around much. The biggest issue was getting up from sitting down, and anytime I had to bend my joints was painful. But once I was up, I could walk and move around. Onstage, holding on to the microphone stand, the crowd had no idea I was struggling with anything.

After the doctor prescribed treatment, she gave me an interesting prognosis: "The way you went to bed and woke up not being able to walk will be the same exact experience when you get over this. You'll wake up one morning as if you never had a problem." Being honest, I absolutely did *not* believe her. I also thought if that were true of the typical person, it certainly wouldn't be for me. When she told me this would magically go away one day, I still thought I was dying. There were many times I sat in that flower chair and cried, thinking, *This is going to be my life now.*

Shannon

Juggling the usual round-the-clock care for Sam with Bart's incapacitating arthritis, I was having to work very hard to not be resentful toward life, often asking myself, *Is this it? Is this as good as it's going to get? Where's the "abundant life," Lord?* Over the years, between being pregnant and raising babies, I was not sleeping more than a couple hours at a time. To manage Sam's diabetes, the insulin we had to administer was different at night, which required checking his blood sugar levels at midnight, 3:00 a.m., and 6:00 a.m. It was tough when those middle-of-the-night alarms would go off. Then, of course, with that many little kids, you might as well stay up and get started with your day after the last early-morning check.

Months later, one random morning, just as the doctor predicted, I woke up, feeling like nothing had ever happened. When my feet hit the floor, I realized I wasn't stiff. In complete shock, I stood and walked. No pain. Normal movement. I was healed! I felt like Charlie's grandfather in the aforementioned chocolate factory movie when he got up out of bed and started dancing because of the golden ticket. I ran around the house like a crazy man, yelling, "It's gone! There's nothing wrong!" I also thought of all the people Jesus instantly healed and how I could now relate to that feeling.

■

In 2011, another fire came that didn't just keep me in the flower chair but strapped me in. And this time, it wasn't just a metaphor, but literal.

My mom had a twin sister who had a son named Todd, a firefighter in Dallas. As first cousins, we were extremely close. Todd was more like having another brother. One day, out on a call where he was in command, Todd and a rookie on his crew were up on the roof of a building that was on fire because they needed to punch a hole to ventilate and prevent backdraft. When they broke through, the roof gave way. Reacting instinctively, Todd pushed the rookie out of the way just before he fell through. It took so long for the other firefighters to reach Todd that, even though they managed to get him to the hospital, he didn't make it. My cousin was killed in the line of duty.

Fortunately, I wasn't on the road. Rushing to the hospital, I walked in to find the hallway lined with firefighters. As I spoke with them all, each one had a story about Todd. With all of us reeling from the news of his death, I stood there and listened to his fellow first responders honor his legacy. That was one of the most disturbing yet proud moments of my life. By now, I thought I would have become accustomed to losing loved ones, maybe even somewhat numb. But each relationship and circumstance was unique and caused me to go through something different. Out of that tragedy, I wrote "The Hurt and The Healer."

Shannon

When Todd died in the fire, his death brought Bart another major setback in his grief, depression, struggles, and questions. Now that Sam was nine years old and Gracie was seven, they were getting old enough and smart enough to pay attention and take notice of our family dynamics that had easily gone over their heads in earlier years. I began to detect some signs that they were starting to resent their dad. When kids are toddlers, you can fake life at home and make it seem like a great day. But Sam and Gracie were starting to pick up on things and also compare us to our friends.

We were in a group of five couples who were all very close with kids around the same ages. The other dads worked Monday through Friday, nine-to-five jobs, which meant they were at every ball game, at every event, and at church with their families on Sunday. With most of Bart's shows on weekends, he was rarely at home on any Saturday for games or Sunday for church. My kids started to take notice that their dad was the only one absent. Frequently, I would plead with Bart, "When you're home, I need you to show up. The kids are growing up fast. I need you to be present. They need you to be present." Especially after Todd's death, Bart's two modes were to ignore me or give me something that sounded hopeful but wasn't going to happen.

My biggest fear and concern became that, as the kids grew into teenagers and young adults, they were going to hate Bart *and* Jesus, the two men they needed the most now and throughout their entire lives. I credit my tribe of friends and family for getting us through all those terrible years with each of them having a hand in saving us. Whoever said it takes a village to raise a child was right!

Earlier, I mentioned my struggle with being the only one in the band who could never miss a show or a media event. But anytime I would think about hanging it up, I would quickly feel guilty and responsible for all the people who would be out of work if I did. There were more than a few blow-up arguments with Brickell about that dilemma. In my venting to him, I would say things like "I can't get sick! I can't lose my voice! I can't quit!"

Not long after Todd's death, this issue finally came to a head. Mike and Abby Scheuchzer asked to meet with the band to tell us they wanted to adopt a child in Kazakhstan. (Located in central Asia, bordering both Russia and China, it's the ninth-largest country in the world in land mass.) To satisfy that country's foreign adoption laws, as is true in many nations, their family would have to go there to live for weeks. The entire process required being legally vetted and approved, granted the right to adopt a child, and then receiving the child into your family, allowing them to monitor everyone. All this had to take place for the government to let you take one of their children out of the country. This commitment and process would cause Mike to be away from the band for around three months. We all knew we would need to find a reliable replacement on guitar and backing vocals for that time. Still, life for MercyMe would go on as scheduled.

Because of both the length of time Mike would be gone and the fact that this was one of us putting family over the band, my anger about my role began to produce bitterness in my heart. The seed of resentment had definitely taken root. My thoughts were bombarded with *Mike can just walk away and go adopt a daughter! I couldn't possibly do that even if Shannon and I wanted to!* I'm sure you're way ahead of me, but I was not at all focused on the blessing to both Mike's family and precious little Millie, the beautiful girl they ended up adopting and bringing home. I wasn't rejoicing *for* them, but feeling envy *of* them.

I started feeling a conviction about how unhealthy this mindset was and how my attitude was detrimental to my own mental, emotional, and spiritual well-being.

Funny how we typically think the issue is with someone else when we are clearly the owner of the problem. Battling all those toxic feelings, I began to realize that something had to be seriously wrong with me, especially with Mike being a lifelong friend and partner in the band. I started feeling a conviction about how unhealthy this mindset was and how my attitude was detrimental to my own mental, emotional, and spiritual well-being.

Shannon

When Bart began to voice his feelings to me about Mike leaving for several months, he was still at the place of saying yes to everything for MercyMe so he could be gone. He was living out his "Do more" mantra. Talking out our feelings about the band brought about the worst time in our marriage. Everything wrong was peaking to create a crossroads moment. At least when we had dealt with family members dying, Bart and I were connected in our grief. With this, we weren't connected at all. I already felt like my husband was disappearing while I carried everything. Because we had agreed to having all these little people in our house, I wanted him to show up and be part of their lives. This situation with the band just exacerbated all those dynamics and gave me more reasons to see why he wasn't around for our family.

Even though everyone had agreed for Mike to go and they would hire a sub, the realization that any of the other guys could do this except Bart set fire to an already smoldering issue. When he told me the plan, on the one hand, as a mom and as a friend to the Scheuchzers, I thought, *Wow, that's amazing. I'm so glad for them.* But on the other hand, with my feelings about the MercyMe machine, I joined Bart's attitude: *If we wanted to adopt a baby in a foreign country, we couldn't just shut the band down for months!*

Being embarrassingly transparent, Bart and I started to fuel each other's resentment. Our discussion escalated to the place of saying, "Our family is always the one paying the highest price and making the biggest sacrifice." As the supportive wife, I added, "Bart, you have to be at everything with the band, even things the other guys don't have to do. There are many days when you have to go take care of some commitment while they're off and at home with their families."

Normally, I could stay even-keeled and help Bart reason something out, but on this specific issue, I didn't help at all. I was not a good encourager toward peace and resolve. In fact, I came to the conclusion that if you're going to call yourself a band, then everybody has to play equal roles with equal sacrifice. I could see that the weight of this internal battle was on the verge of causing Bart to crash and burn.

Following Todd's death and now my feelings about Mike's absence, I finally came to the place of admitting ...

"I'm tired of having to sing at funerals."
"I'm so tired of singing 'Imagine' at funerals."
"I don't want to be the lead singer of a band anymore."

After Mike got home and came back to work, Shannon and I had a heart-to-heart to get on the same page. After that, I called a meeting with the guys and told them, "I can't do this anymore. Shannon is with me on this. She just wants me to get healthy. We need to talk about an ending."

The guys heard me out and then collectively asked, "Can we talk this out and see if we can fix what's broken?"

Shannon

Bart finally hit the wall, came to a decision, and told me he had called a band meeting. He said he was going to simply tell them, "I quit. I'm done. I'm out. I can't carry this pressure any longer." Part of me thought, *Yes! Finally!* Then the other side of me was thinking, *Okay, but what are we going to do next? This is all we've ever known.*

When the guys in the band heard Bart's surprise resignation, they responded, "Whoa! Can we try and fix this?" Feeling like he owed them all the opportunity to hear them out, Bart agreed and listened. My feelings were that I wanted to be supportive of my husband as long as some real and lasting changes would be made.

When the guys asked me what I wanted, at the time we were playing 175 shows a year. I told them, "I want to cut back to 60 a year." I really thought they would think that was crazy and it wouldn't work.

To my surprise, they all responded, "Okay, if that's what it takes."

Totally shocked, I came back, "Wait, what? ... For real?!"

They assured me they weren't bluffing. This was just as serious to them as it was to me. The fact that they were willing to agree to some sacrifices and make the necessary changes with me was such a huge relief and encouragement.

That solidarity was a major turning point for both MercyMe and the Millard family.

Chapter 6

THE HARD WORK OF HEALING

Shannon

Bart came home from the band meeting and told me about their response. What I anticipated to be a report of how everything would be wrapped up had become a very possible decision to keep going, but drastically cut back on the days away from home. While I have always loved the other guys and their families, by this point, I was very weary of the machine that MercyMe had become. To explain this dynamic through a business or corporate filter, it's the difference in the relationships between coworkers versus the unhealthy dynamics the company can create. But when Bart told me the changes everyone was willing to make, I responded, "Okay, great, then let's reset everything." My bottom line was wanting real solutions, and this sounded like they were all in agreement to find the balance.

Looking back, 2005 to 2011 had been a blur. Because I was consumed with having babies and raising children, I struggle to recall many details. My grief and depression, alongside Bart's, made the days drag and the years fly. By 2012, with five kids, the fighter in me was wanting to get up off the mat and try to go another round. Taking a deep-dive personal inventory, I admitted to myself, *I can't do this anymore. The burden is just too heavy. I want to be healthy mentally, emotionally, spiritually, and physically. Nothing's going to hold me back and keep me down any longer.*

Exhausted from trying to keep Band-Aids on shrapnel wounds, I knew it was time for me to find some real answers. I knew I would have to start by going back to Chris's death and deal with that event in the right way. From there, I would have to move forward through all the trauma. I wanted to find a solid Christian counselor, a woman whom I could feel comfortable opening up to about all the gory details of my life. While I wasn't placing the blame on anyone for what had happened in the past, I had to take responsibility for where I was going in the future. I was ready to take action toward a positive outcome.

Engaging my investigative skills again, I had a good feeling about one certain counselor whose name was Adora and made my first appointment with her. In my early sessions, the more I shared, the more I uncovered and the more I discovered. The more truth that came out, the better I felt. Light was once again starting to pour into my soul. In my opinion, there are two major reliefs that can come through the right counseling: First, you open up and spill your guts with no filter, getting 100 percent honest—something most of us desperately need to do, but don't or won't. The things we hold in and keep secret are the very things that can kill us. That's why Bart and I were slowly dying. Second, as you begin to find real answers, you can acquire tools to not just get back to where you were before the fire came but to an even better, healthier place. That is always God's goal as He transforms us into the image of Jesus. There are times when we need professional help to get back to that journey and find our path again.

After a while, Adora started saying, "You know, Shannon, Bart really needs to come see me too." My answer was always the same: "Yeah, I know, but he won't." Finally, one day, I told her I had come up with a plan that just might work. While I suppose you could call this a soft intervention or even downright misleading, I know that, ultimately, this was for my husband's own good and our family's good.

That night, I said, "Hey, Bart, my counselor wants you to come in with me to my next appointment and tell her how you think I'm doing." He looked a bit surprised and asked, "So, kind of like a progress report on you?" I answered, "Sure ... We should take two cars so you can leave when you need to." I know my husband well. Bart took the bait—hook, line, and sinker.

At the appointment, Adora began to lob Bart a few softball questions. Just as I suspected, he started talking, opening up to her about his dad and his childhood. Let's just say he backed the truck up and began to unload baggage, just as I had prayed would happen. As he continued to share with her, I saw my moment and quietly excused myself to "go to the restroom." Whispering to Bart to keep going, I walked out the door to my car and drove home.

By the end of the session, when time was up, the counselor told me that Bart asked, "Hey, this was good. Can we do it again?"

Mission accomplished.

Shannon had first told me that she was going to see a counselor to try to deal with the loss of her brother. At that time, she knew there was no way I would agree to go. One day, Shannon asked me to come sit in on her session to talk about the progress she had made. She told me there were some things she wanted to say to me with the counselor. I agreed to go solely to support my wife. At one point, when I was talking, Shannon said she needed to go to the restroom. And, yes, just as she told you, she never came back. But, honestly, I didn't notice. I had no idea I had been ambushed. My wife had decided that would be the only way to get me into the office. All the counselor had to do was ask a question about my childhood and I opened up. Shannon knew I had needed someone to talk to for so long and it wouldn't take much to get me going. At the end of that session, I asked when I could come back. Starting that day, my willingness to get help gave Shannon hope to believe that we could be on a healing journey together.

Shannon

By the time Bart got started with his own counseling, I was already thriving in my experience and thought it was amazing. But because there was so much trauma from his childhood, teenage years, and the past several years that he hadn't dealt with, Bart was confessing, "I'm dying here. Please don't make me go anymore." While we couldn't have been more opposite in our response to counseling at first, it didn't take long before Bart began to discover the same truths that I did. He started to experience real healing from his past, and his progress was amazing.

After Adora began helping Bart uncover various issues, he started sharing past situations with me that I never knew about, some of which ended up in the first movie and book. I began to understand so much more of what he had been doing at home, or not doing at home, that now made total sense. They all involved deep emotional triggers from his past. Now, the "whats" were being explained as the "whys" were unearthed.

There were so many things he had hidden over the years through making jokes or giving disguised excuses. One example was when we were kids, our friend group never once went to Bart's house. I just assumed that Arthur (Bart's dad) didn't want us there. All these years later, Bart finally confessed to me that he wasn't sure what his dad might do, and he couldn't take any chances with being embarrassed or belittled in front of us, so he constantly made up reasons why we didn't need to go to his house. Or, even if his dad wasn't home, he didn't want anyone to see the mess that three guys created.

With both of us going to counseling, individually and together, we were able to finally stop treating the symptoms and start dealing with the actual source of the problems. We also went to several intensive weekends. One particular marathon session was seven hours. So much good came from every minute we invested in our marriage and our family. What we also discovered was, while of course we had our personal and marital issues, so much of what had come at us was from external sources—deaths and disease we had no say in or control over.

Once Shannon and I began to open up the can of worms we had kept the lid on for too long, we realized what horrible shape we were in. Kind of like you can know at the accident site that your car is probably totaled, but once you take a good look at it in the body shop, the reality of the damage and what you survived starts to sink in. I had finally come to the place of admitting, "I need to fix myself and we need to fix us." Songs like "Dear Younger Me" came out of those sessions as I began to connect my childhood to who I am as an adult, husband, and father.

For Shannon, the biggest blessing and answer to prayer was all about me finally proving to her that our marriage and family were worth fighting for. As with all counseling, there were some amazing sessions and then some really painful times. But we had never been closer after starting to go through our baggage together. Thank God Shannon found the right help and that I can say today, while I'm nowhere near arriving, I am at the healthiest place I've ever been. I have also become a major advocate for Christian counseling. (Oh, and we began to refer to our counselor as Adora, the Mind Explorer, our own personal version of *Dora the Explorer*.)

Starting that day, my willingness to get help gave Shannon hope to believe that we could be on a healing journey together.

Going back to the band and the new chapter we were working toward, one realization was that the other guys had no connection to Texas like I did. I had never asked them to move to the Dallas area. Being the first one to get married, I had told them, "Because both our families are in Greenville, I'm going to live there to be close to everyone." Each band member had chosen to follow suit, so we all lived in the same area. That decision had made the logistics of leaving and coming home easier as we had the same home base. With the decision to cut back on shows, the question naturally arose, "Is this the beginning of the end?" For the first time, there was a major shift in thinking about the band's future.

When Barry joined as an official member, he had chosen to leave Nashville to move to Texas. We had met him when he was playing guitar for several different Christian artists. He was the first one to decide that if we should call it quits, he wanted to be in the best possible place to keep working as a musician. After agreeing together as a band, Barry and his family left Dallas to move back to Nashville, where all of MercyMe's team was anyway. Soon after, Mike and his family made the call to move to Nashville for the same reasons.

I never thought Greenville would be the final destination for any of us. For years, we had all talked and dreamed out loud of someday making the move to Music City. In 1996, as a new band with all of us single, back when Brickell first started trying to help us get a record deal, we had briefly lived in Nashville. But now, with everyone having a family, there was so much more at stake. Everything was different. I felt like, for so many years, the guys had made a sacrifice for me to live near my family. Had any of them decided at any point that they needed to move elsewhere, I would have blessed their decision. The fact that they were either moving or contemplating a move now gave Shannon and me the nudge to tell them,

"Hey, guys, if Nashville is where you want to be, then we want to be team players like you all have been." I think we all began to feel like if we were ever going to make the move, now was the time. Change was definitely our new theme as a band.

For so many years, had any of these changes taken place or had the band broken up, it would have destroyed me, because my life and identity were totally wrapped up in MercyMe. Through all the intensive counseling, I had been able to arrive at a place where I was confident everything would be okay with or without the band. For everything except my family, I was learning the freedom of holding on to things loosely. Whatever the next steps might be, I knew we were going to be good. As I talked through the future with Adora, her primary encouragement was "Whatever you decide to do, keep it healthy and in balance."

Now, with so much change happening, there was still one major part of my life that had to be addressed.

■

For so many people, an ongoing battle with grief and depression over years either causes extreme weight loss or weight gain. Coupled with my sedentary lifestyle of sitting in the flower chair over all those years at home and the rest of my time living on a bus, my health had been seriously affected. In December of 2012, I turned forty. Early in 2013, I finally made the tough call to go see my doctor, whom I had known for a long time.

The results of the visit were not good. My weight was around 370 pounds. My blood pressure was high. Cholesterol was high. All my lipid panel numbers were horrible. I was prediabetic and struggling with sleep apnea. After my doctor went through the list, he stated, "Bart, you have every red flag known to man. Your dad died at the age of forty-eight, but you won't make it to that age unless we take action now. I want to keep you alive, so next week you're going in to have gastric bypass surgery. Normally, there's several months of preparation and counseling required. We'll try to get insurance to cover it, but we cannot waste any more time. You have the money now, so I'm telling you, you can't afford to *not* do this. We have to start to turn your health around *today*."

My doctor's tone and determination made it clear that he was not going to budge or leave this decision open for discussion. He literally treated me like someone who had come into the ER and was going to need to go immediately to surgery to save my life. He was urgent in a way I had never seen before. Today, I'm so grateful he made the call for me when I didn't have the will or the energy.

Following the successful surgery, I dropped 130 pounds. Everything—blood pressure, prediabetes, bad blood numbers, and apnea—reversed and returned to normal. Thanks to my doctor, my health did indeed turn around. Heading into my forties, the surgery, along with counseling and changes in the band, was launching me into a complete life reset. The first real positive step for me in far too long.

Shannon

After so much progress and healing, Bart and I began a conversation with our counselor on what next steps might look like for us to move forward in health as a family. The three of us agreed that leaving Greenville would be a strong step. Whether we went to Nashville or not, we were ready for a major change. While our hometown would forever be the place we met, married, had our kids, and lived among such great family and friends, there would always be the other side too.

This would always be where Bart had silently endured abuse as a child and teenager, where my brother died, where Uncle Rick died, where Todd died, and where Sam had been diagnosed with diabetes. Had we made the decision to leave our home before, we would have been running. The problem with that choice is you just take all the issues with you. But a move amid our reset would offer a fresh start.

While the other guys in MercyMe were already there or seriously considering Nashville, it was the one place that was like a second home to Bart. MercyMe's management, booking agency, record label, tour support, recording studios, and songwriting base were there. If his work was in Music City, that made the most practical sense as the destination for our family. Aside from when he was on tour, living there would allow his songwriting, album production, and business meetings to be a short commute, not a planned trip away.

For me, this move was only about one thing: saving our family. For us to get to a healthy place, if I had to leave everything and not look back, I would. The ultimate win for me and the kids would be more time with all seven of us, not just six of us. We could also be around other musicians' families who have never lived in the nine-to-five world. My kids could relate to and better understand their dad's world. Just as Sam and Gracie had compared their dad to fathers with normal jobs and schedules in Texas, now the playing field could be more level.

As a wife and mom, this goes back to my primary goal of doing everything possible for my kids to love their dad and Jesus. Our whole family would start over together. Our counselor's advice was "When you don't have any regrets in leaving, that's when you know you can leave." Because of so many family members and friends in Texas, I wasn't sure I would ever reach the perfect place to say that, but I was as close as I would ever be.

Bart and I agreed the move would be hard but we were ready to experience that struggle together. We wanted to create our own unique family memories, for all of us to be closer, to experience life with just the seven of us. I thought about Abram and his family in Genesis 12:1: "The LORD had said to Abram, 'Go from your country, your people and your father's household to the land I will show you.'" Going to Bart's "country" now, where we didn't know anyone, he was going to help carry us.

Lining out the details of our move, Bart and I began to feel excitement for the first time in years about starting over and struggling together, not separately. Our entire lives, we had been part of a tribe constantly doing everything together. Even in our worst days of struggle, we always had a safety net below us, knowing that no matter what happened, it was never a question of *if* someone would show up to help, but *how many*. Obviously, in moving, we were cutting the net and leaving everyone behind.

Shannon was the first to actually say, "Maybe we should move to Nashville too?" When I asked, "For real? Are you sure?" she answered, "I know it's going to be really hard and it's against everything I've wanted, but we desperately need the change." One hundred percent, she made our move happen. While the final decision was made together, if she had never brought up the idea, we wouldn't have left.

By the end of summer in 2013, everyone except Robby, our drummer, had moved to Nashville. He and his family decided to stay in Texas and he would work out travel arrangements just like we always had before. Everyone in MercyMe was so gracious and, to this day, we have all been true to our agreement, with our individual and corporate health being first priority.

In August that year, we made our move. As we headed east to Franklin, Tennessee (a southern suburb of Nashville), where much of the Christian music industry has always been based, Texas slowly disappeared in the rearview mirror. We were leaving our huge support system to learn to rely only on each other, to do life 100 percent together as a family, just us with our five kids.

For the first time, the Millard family abandoned the comfort zone of being settlers and ventured out as trailblazers.

Chapter 7

ALL WE HAVE IS EACH OTHER

Shannon

On our move to Tennessee, Bart and I made the decision to rent to allow ourselves time to scope out the area and get the lay of the land before making a decision to buy or build a home. The first two years in the house we leased, our only neighbors were horses, cows, and our landlord, whose home was several acres over from ours. To say we went through culture shock would be a major understatement. We went from knowing everyone to knowing only a handful of people, from constantly being around a large tribe of family and friends to just the seven of us.

At the time we left Texas, our youngest son, Miles, was two. He and my dad were best buddies. They were together all the time. So after the move, every single day, Miles would ask to see his Papa. I just kept telling myself, *This is what I have to do for our family.* I knew I couldn't turn back. If I did, I could be risking my marriage. So, to use Bart's rearview mirror metaphor, I had to rip mine off the car, so the only direction I could look was forward.

A while later, my friends back home told me, "We were concerned because we didn't hear from you for a long time." I responded, "I know, because I couldn't bear talking with you. I gave everything up to save our family and sacrifice my old life for a new one." Being in the music industry for so long, Bart already knew a lot of folks in Nashville. While I had met a few over the years here and there, I had no close friends to lean on. I quickly figured out that it's easy to talk about knowing what you have when you're in the middle of it, but once we moved, we truly did have a full appreciation for the love and support we had received from family and friends for so long. Now, by ourselves, we could clearly see the village we once had around us, which gave us even more gratitude for everyone back in Greenville.

It's like when you sing a worship song that says, "Break my heart, oh God." You can't fully understand what you're asking for until you experience a broken heart. We have to be careful what we pray. We can say we want the struggle, but then once we're in it, we question, "Dear Lord, what did we do?" There were definitely some moments when Bart and I looked at each other and asked that very question. When you're surrounded by a beautiful community, it's easy to lean on them. Now, we only had each other, which quickly began to create a deeper bond. That was the beauty of the choice we had made and what we hoped to experience. The gift I most wanted was for us to be a close family.

Sam was twelve when we moved. Back in Greenville, he was Big Man on Campus at his school. Everyone knew him. Because of so much awareness of his diabetes and our family, hundreds of people would participate in sponsored walks to raise money for the cause. We would take part in massive events for diabetes in Dallas. To go from being so well known to knowing no one was very hard on Sam. Without his extended family and friends, he quickly became heartbroken and depressed.

We made the decision to homeschool the kids, based on having to put Sam somewhere we would have no idea how he was doing at any given hour of the day. In a new public or private school, we would no longer have easy access to him and wouldn't yet know anyone to ask how he was doing or check on him. Handing Sam over to a teacher and a school nurse who may not know the risks of type 1 just didn't feel right. Up to this point, I had vowed I would never homeschool, but once we gave it a chance and committed, I soon came to love it.

In mid-September, Bart left on MercyMe's fall tour. Our promise to the kids of "you're going to have more time with Dad" suddenly seemed like a bait and switch. For them and me, we had left all the things we loved for more time with Bart. We had our hopes high that life was going to be great, and the kids were trusting us to deliver on that promise. While the band had agreed to do only about a third of the number of shows they had been doing, this tour was still going to be a marathon. But we were baptized by fire. For the next two months of 2013, Bart was only home about ten days total.

■

After the move, one of our first orders of business was to find a new endocrinologist for Sam's care. We asked around and finally got a recommendation we felt might work. At the first visit, the doctor told us, "Sam is thirteen now and in seventh grade. It's time for him to own his disease. You can't wait until he goes off to college or leaves home to hand over all of his care to him. You need to start now."

My response was, "No, no, no, we just had a major life change, and this is horrible timing for all of us." But the doctor dismissed me with an "I'm the expert; I know best" attitude. As Sam's mom, I fully understood a transition would have to take place at some point. That made sense. But up to now, I was still doing everything for him. I realized there was the need for a handoff one day, but I also knew where Sam was emotionally after the move, and he was not in a good place to take everything on yet.

Wanting to listen and trust our new doctor, we decided to abide by his advice. I started the process of handing Sam responsibility of his own care. As I suspected with my mother's-intuition, the sudden transition proved too much. One day, he got very sick with what I thought at first was a virus. But his blood sugar became extremely erratic. For context, a nondiabetic A1c level is 5.56, making that your ultimate goal. Sam had never gotten below 7.5 in Texas, which is considered normal range for a diabetic. His test result was 13.

One of the most life-threatening complications of diabetes is DKA, or diabetic ketoacidosis. According to the American Diabetes Association, "When your cells don't get the glucose they need for energy, your body begins to burn fat for energy, which produces ketones—chemicals that the body creates when it breaks down fat to use for energy. When the body doesn't have enough insulin to use glucose,... ketones build up in the blood ... [and] make it more acidic. High levels of ketones can poison the body. They are a warning sign that your diabetes is out of control or that you are getting sick.... DKA is a serious condition that can lead to a coma or death."[1]

Finding out that result, I was gripped by fear and sadness. The reality was Sam had become apathetic. His loneliness in our transition was causing him to not care about living, much less managing his diabetes. Knowing full well the severity of ketoacidosis, I had said that Sam would never face that on my watch. Being honest, trying every day to be a big girl since our move, I was back at a difficult place myself and struggling emotionally too. Because of that, I had missed Sam's cues that I would have normally caught. In Texas, under normal circumstances, I would have had a much better grasp on his care. At night after the kids were in bed, I would go in my closet, shut the door, curl up on the floor, and sob, asking God, "What have I done?" But the next morning, I would put on my smile, pull up my bootstraps, and ask the kids, "What adventure do you want to go on today?" I would go right back into cheerleader–tour guide mode.

Thank God we got Sam through that crisis and he leveled out again. But at his next checkup, the doctor's expert attitude was on display again. He came into the exam room and scanned Sam's numbers that we had provided. He looked up, stared at us for a moment, then shocked me with his accusation: "These can't possibly be accurate. There's no way you did this."

In disbelief, I shot back, "Yes, we did."

His comeback was even more emphasized. "No ... you didn't."

Trying to process what was happening, I went from surprise to being insulted and infuriated. "Why in the world would we lie about this?! I'm vouching for my son because I watched him do everything. This is what you asked us to do."

But he wouldn't back down and pushed back. "There's no way."

I had gone against my instincts before to try to comply, but these accusations made me realize his arrogance. I stood up and stated, "Sam went into ketoacidosis, which has *never* happened before. And now you're saying that we're lying. We're leaving and will *never* be back here! We're done!"

The doctor's approach was basically the classic horror story of teaching a kid to swim by throwing the child in the deep end to see if they figure out a way to not drown. I had endured the doctor but never liked him. Something about our interactions never felt right. I agreed there was wisdom in Sam needing to own his disease, but I didn't think dumping it on him overnight was the right approach. In spite of my call from God to parent my kids, plus my gut feelings, I had pushed past the red flags, but I learned a valuable lesson to not allow that again. When we walked out of that doctor's office, I had no idea where else to go; I just knew we couldn't stay there. How do you try to come back from a confrontation like that? I had never liked the way he treated Sam or me. He wasn't respectful of the relationship, and that was my final straw, which actually turned out to be a blessing in disguise.

From there, we went to Vanderbilt Children's Hospital in Nashville. After we told them our story and the history of how we came to be there that day, the staff showed us a lot of grace. They loved on us, made us feel so comfortable, and proved we could trust them. They worked with us, not against us, to help get Sam back on track.

When your child has a high-maintenance chronic illness, it is so easy for the relationship to become about only one thing—the disease. The constant care doesn't leave enough room to bond over anything else. For Sam to just go hang out with friends, we had to ask, "Do you have a snack? Do you have your shots? Do you have your insulin?" Life could never be "All right, go have fun!" Because you desperately want a healthy relationship with your child, you work hard for him to not hate you, despise you, and resent you. In the constant work of trying to balance these difficult dynamics, Bart and I just wanted to be Sam's parents.

Months later, when the next checkup rolled around, another snag occurred. We were told we had to switch doctors and got assigned to a new endocrinologist. On this visit, Bart was home and came with me and Sam. The doctor walked in with no real introduction, and after looking at Sam's numbers, she immediately got very strong with us. "You're killing your son. He'll be dead by the time he's nineteen." *Here we go again! Seriously?!* We didn't know what to do or say. Feeling like we had been here before, I definitely got mad at her words and approach. This time, the accusation was that we were withdrawn parents. I already had one doctor treat me this way, so I wasn't going to put up with another. My eyes began to well up with tears of pure anger. We were all upset by another round of what could only feel like condemnation.

After another confrontational appointment, I knew I had to take some time to think through and pray about what to do. After all, Sam was not a kid anymore where Bart could hold his arms and I could give him the shot. Like us, he had heard and understood the doctor's concerns. He could voice whatever he felt about his situation and us as his parents. Miraculously, with the new doctor, we managed to get past the upset of that initial meeting. Over time, getting to know one another, she turned out to become a dear friend and we were able to see that her first response was only out of protection for Sam. No one knows better than an endocrinologist that mismanagement of type 1 can lead to debilitating conditions and even death.

The toughest realization was knowing we had no choice but to get tougher on Sam. I had to arrive at the conclusion that he may end up hating us, but at least we would still have him. After losing my brother, I knew I would rather have a loved one hate me than be gone forever. This decision was going to mean a lot more fighting and arguing with our teenage son.

Sam

Because I was diagnosed with type 1 diabetes as a toddler, this was my life, all I've ever known. I've heard my parents tell the story that it's a miracle I'm even here, so I'm grateful they were able to catch the symptoms, get my blood sugar under control, and figure out what was going on.

After we moved to Nashville, there were a lot of fights over the transition of me trying to take care of myself. Living in fear every day of doing something wrong in my care was really tough on everyone. When my parents were handling everything, I just had to sit and watch it all. But as I was coming into my teen years, I began to realize this was *my* life—a life I had *no* control over. It's strange when normal is overwhelming. Regardless of my age, having to do math for how much insulin to take just because I wanted a snack *never* got any easier.

By the time they started giving me control, I was angry that I had to deal with diabetes at all. I began to question, "Do I really need this? Is this even real?" I was definitely a typical teen boy. I'll admit I was very stubborn. One day, I decided to not take my medication just to see what would happen. I wanted to test the waters, which is the dumbest thing you can do as a diabetic. I lied when my parents asked, "Did you take a shot?" I hadn't, but answered yes, saying, "It's fine. Don't worry about it."

I ended up in the ER and almost died. My wake-up call regarding my diabetes was literally waking up in the hospital. I realized this was *very* real, a too-close call I will never forget that definitely produced some trauma for me.

The next couple years were still a battle as I went through puberty, which, to no surprise, caused its own issues. Those years are hard enough for kids and parents, even without diabetes. I had to deal with blood sugar spikes and a roller-coaster ride of moving numbers. That was back when we didn't have the sensors that constantly monitor my numbers. Today, I have access to lifesaving technology, but back then it was still the "prick your finger, draw blood, and read the numbers" method.

As a teenager, the more my parents and I argued, the more I felt like the blame was being placed on me and the more rebellious I felt. Yet there were enough factors out of my control that I didn't feel fully to blame. We fought to the point where I know Mom and Dad were tempted to just let it go. At one point, I remember them telling me, "Of course we care, but we're so tired of fighting you for control." Honestly, at that point, I felt like no one had control over my condition. One example of that happened when I was fifteen. I had a seizure one night in my sleep. Once again, I woke up in the ER, which was so frustrating. Even when I thought I was working hard to take care of myself the right way, something like that would happen. For a long time, I felt like nothing about my life was fair.

There are times in life when the hardest decisions you ever make, that start out as the toughest to endure, turn out to be the best ones in the long run.

In Nashville, we got every bit of what we asked for—and more. From the initial transition and struggle with feeling lonely and isolated, along with the difficult doctors' appointments and ER visits, the hard times we knew we had signed up for definitely came. But there are times in life when the hardest decisions you ever make, that start out as the toughest to endure, turn out to be the best ones in the long run. Looking back today, we know we definitely made the right call. Our move to reset was the best thing that ever happened to our family because, through all the trials, over time, the seven of us got closer than ever. Exactly Shannon's prayer. With me being home more now than ever in our history, it was just us. Moving away from our safety net in Texas and all the tragedies we had experienced there was indeed good for us.

The kind of good God promises when we follow where He leads.

THE REAL HEROES IN THIS STORY

Between Shannon, her mom, and my mom, there was a definite "girl power" vibe in our family. The three of them had an undeniable synergy to take care of business and get things done. Through everything our family went through, those three held down the fort while I was on the road in those high-demand years of MercyMe, all while navigating the trials.

After the *I Can Only Imagine* movie came out, many of the most consistent questions everyone asked me were about my mom: "What was the deal with her?" "Where did she go?" "Did you ever see her again?" "What happened to her?" In the movie, to condense the story, my mom dropped me off at children's camp and then never came back, leaving me alone with my dad and brother. In the first book I was able to tell the full story, which wasn't as brutal as that scene made it look. She did leave Dad and didn't take Stephen and me, but she didn't just disappear. Over the years, my brother and I did see her from time to time. In later years, Mom and I were able to restore our relationship. Before the first movie came out, I was able to sit with her and watch it, so she could see the story for herself.

After Mom's last husband died, she ended up moving back to Greenville to be near us. When any family crisis occurred—like when Chris died and Sam was diagnosed—my mom (Nana) was right there helping any way she could. She may have had a lot of faults, but she was all in as a caregiver who was good at being present to do whatever was needed. When Frank was in surgery with the brain tumor, Mom was right there with the rest of the family in the waiting room. If anyone was in the hospital, provided she could get to Dallas, she would come for support. After each one of our babies was born, she was at the house waiting when we got home. Whether she was serving or sitting with us, Mom was always there. While she wasn't necessarily good at engaging and playing with the kids, anytime there was a need or crisis, Mom was the first one to show up and the last one to leave.

Yet, because she was never there for me growing up, as an adult, for some reason I made up my mind that she still wasn't there. As they say, perception is reality. A mixture of past emotions and unforgiveness wouldn't allow me to acknowledge that she was there for us now. Once we started having kids, I would complain to Shannon how Mom wasn't the grandmother I wanted her to be. When Mom and I finally talked everything out, made things right, and found a healthy balance, the pressure was off both of us. I don't think she ever knew the expectation I placed on her; honestly, something she simply wasn't capable of. When I finally let all that go, our relationship got so much better and I started seeing the person Mom actually was. My complaining stopped and my acceptance began. The irony was that the same dynamic of expectation I had run from for years, I had been placing on my own mother.

Sadly, I didn't fully appreciate my mom until she had a seizure and was placed in a convalescent facility to recover. While there, she had some mini-strokes, which caused her health to decline rapidly. The doctors informed us she had very little brain capacity left and was barely hanging on. By this point, our family had moved to Tennessee. Getting that news, we made the drive back to Texas to be with her. My brother's family lived near Mom, so they were always nearby.

When I arrived and walked into Mom's room, I saw her lying in the hospital bed, her eyes blank, staring nowhere. When I tried to talk to her, the other family members said, "Bart, she can't hear you. She's gone." But because her heart was still beating, the doctor said she had a little brain activity left, and her eyes were open, so I was holding out hope.

That night, as everyone began to leave to go home, I decided I would stay with her. For the next three to four hours, I sat by Mom's bedside. I had seen and heard enough stories about how someone in that state may actually be able to hear you. Not knowing how much time I might have left with Mom, I decided to start talking to her. Feeling like I was on the clock, I was trying to think of everything I needed to say, anything I would want her to hear for closure. I opened up about all the times I had been hurt, angry, and frustrated with her. But then I also let her know how much I loved her and had desperately wanted to be with her as a kid. As I said, years before, we had reconciled enough to restart our relationship, but on that night, I knew I had to get *everything* out. The entire time I shared my heart, she showed no sign of life.

Someone in the family had brought in a small speaker and had been playing MercyMe songs in her room. Over the past several years, she had been our number one fan, so they wanted to play her favorite songs. That made me think back to the first album that Mom ever bought me as a kid—Leo Sayer's 1976 *Endless Flight*. I played it so much that I had every song memorized. It's still one of my favorite vinyls today. There were two massive hits on that record that became classics. One was "You Make Me Feel Like Dancing."

I decided to pull that album up on my phone and play the other hit song, "When I Need You." As I sat there taking in the words that were actually quite fitting in this moment, I looked over at Mom to see a tear rolling out of the corner of her eye down her face. With no movement, that single tear told me that my mother must have heard every word I had said that evening. The fact that I ended my final time alone with her by playing one of our favorite songs touched something deep inside her mother's-heart. Even though her body was in its final hours and her mind was unable to produce words, her spirit was still very much alive.

The next night, as everyone was leaving, knowing Mom didn't have long, my brother Stephen and I decided to stay the night. We began to reminisce and talk about growing up, sharing funny moments and hard memories. During those few hours, I felt a sense of peace. That time with my brother, in the presence of our mom, will always be very special to me. Around 5:00 a.m., after Stephen and I had finally drifted off to sleep, Mom quietly slipped away. I woke to the sound of her taking one deep, final breath. After watching her for a few minutes, I checked her pulse. She was gone.

For so long, I assumed I probably wouldn't be there when Mom passed away. I would likely be out on the road somewhere or not be able to get from Tennessee to Texas in time. The fact that I was able to be with her and the family the entire time, and even be with her when she passed, was such a blessing of God's timing that I will always be grateful for.

Mom passed away on July 6, 2022. In those final years, she and Claudette, Shannon's mom, were best friends. Everything they had both gone through forged an undeniable bond, from experiencing the joy of grandbabies born to the sadness of loved ones lost.

During a 2025 podcast interview, the host asked me a question about my mom. I shared how she had never learned how to take care of Sam. We tried to teach her, but she couldn't seem to get it down, which led to my complaints: "Why can't she learn? Why can't she do it?" Yet, when Shannon's mom would be taking care of Sam, my mom would be right beside her, assisting any way she could. Wrapping up my answer, I said, "It's hard to describe the role my mom played."

The host said, "Well, it sounds like she was Aaron holding up Moses's arms." When I heard that explanation, immediately, I could picture that image and wasn't able to hold back the tears. That was it. That was their relationship. That was exactly the dynamic between our moms. Claudette was like Moses and Dell was like Aaron. Between the two of them, God was glorified and so much ministry was accomplished.

That story of Moses and Aaron has been an ongoing thread for Shannon and me over the years. God has used that example many times in so many circumstances. The truth is, Aaron's role was just as important as Moses's. The proof was how Claudette would always say, "Well, I couldn't do it without Dell." All that time, Mom was holding up her best friend's arms.

Shannon

On her deathbed, Dell was obviously waiting for both of her sons to be there, with no one else around, before she passed. The odds of the three of them being together on her last night on this earth were slim. For that to be exactly what happened was miraculous.

Bart needed closure and to be present during that time. The Lord knew he did and made sure it happened.

After Nana passed away that morning, because of everything we had to do right away, it slipped my mind to call my own mother. Later, when I did reach out with the news, she was devastated. Wanting to be there to say goodbye, she kept saying, "Dell is one of my best friends." The truth is, our moms were best friends. For quite a while, Bart and I had underestimated that fact. Over the years, their relationship grew to be very strong, and we're grateful God blessed our family with them both.

The real heroes of my story are the three women in my life—Shannon, my mother-in-law Claudette, and my mom Dell. They took on the dirty jobs, the toughest behind-the-scenes roles, staying in the background, never receiving the credit they deserved. I knew I had to honor them in these pages.

Chapter 8

GIVING UP THE FIGHT

After years of counseling, a renewed commitment to my health, and the reinvention of MercyMe, there was one more significant change in my life that was desperately needed and began to take shape in this season. One that, at the time, I didn't even realize was missing. My mental, emotional, and physical health had been addressed, and now my spiritual life needed attention. I touched on this story briefly in the first book, but I want to dive into the details here. This aspect became a crucial part of the transformation Shannon and I went through as we recovered and were restored through all the tragedies and trauma.

The main reason I want to share this part of my journey is because of the potential for God to change others' lives as well, especially anyone with a past similar to mine. Most often, anything of any real significance that happens in our lives is connected to a key relationship. So many of our redemptive stories start with "I met a guy who …" or "There was this woman who …" Mine is no different.

Rusty Kennedy is a pastor I have known for many years. He's a friend of the band who we met at one of our first youth camps where we led worship. Over the years, Rusty has hit us up and asked to come out on the road for the weekend when a bunk was available on the bus. As we started the 2013 tour, he had reached out to one of the other guys and asked about going with us for a few days and, of course, we agreed.

The first day out, in conversations with everyone, Rusty began talking through a lot of Scriptures. While I listened, I saw myself as a third party who happened to be in the room. That is, until he made a statement about God's grace that grabbed my attention. Turning to him, I asked, "Now, wait a minute, Rusty. Why would you say that? Where is that coming from?"

That moment was the launching pad for what was about to radically change my entire worldview.

Considering everything I have confessed to you thus far, it's safe to say, had Rusty just come out and stated, "Hey, Bart, I believe I'm out here this weekend because there are some things about God's grace I want to help you understand," that would not have gone well. I wouldn't have received him at all. But after I started asking questions, Rusty and I spent the rest of that trip talking in-depth about some of the truths in the Bible he had recently discovered in a fresh, new way. He ended up coming out on the road with us for a couple more weekends, and from there we started a text thread to keep our conversation going.

Rusty was the first person to tell me what Scripture says about our identity in Christ and help me understand the *biblical* concept of grace. I will never forget him telling me, "Man, Bart, you've been living in this legalistic system of 'doing good better than you do bad.' The problem is, yes, some days you're going to win, but what do you do on the days where you lose? You're keeping score when Jesus isn't. In fact, because of the cross, there is no score to be kept. On your worst possible day, Jesus still loves you and is pleased with you. There is nothing you could do to make Him love you any more than He does right now." Hearing about God's love in that way was like stumbling on an oasis with a shade tree and a pool of fresh water after years of wandering in the desert. I had *never* heard anyone say anything like that before.

In my journey with Rusty, I began to discover a brand-new relationship with Jesus, thirsting and hungering for more. We poured over Scripture to learn about our identity in Christ, which is so much of what the apostle Paul taught in his letters. Having been a religious zealot who focused solely on keeping the Law to the point of hunting down Christians, Saul-turned-Paul had a lot to say about who we are in sin versus who we are in Jesus. He spoke from firsthand experience and revelation. Of course, I had read the New Testament many times, but somehow, I had missed the true meaning behind the message.

The best way I can describe my fresh understanding of New Testament teaching is *awakening*. And I don't use that word to sound spiritual but to describe the reality of how I felt. I had been sleepwalking in my faith for so long and was being shaken awake. All the roles in my life, including my career as an artist and songwriter, began to take a back seat to who I am in Christ. I genuinely reached the point of saying, "My true identity as a child of God no longer has any reliance on a stage and a microphone. Concerts, records, awards, movies, and books are great, but they do not make me who I am."

■

Rusty's own spiritual journey in understanding God's grace came when he was a youth pastor at a little Baptist church in Texas in the '90s. He had decided to take part in joining the thousands of churches who were initiating the True Love Waits program, an abstinence-based teaching for teens. One of the dads who had always been very supportive of Rusty's ministry came to him and politely said, "Hey, let me know when you're done with this study, and I'll bring my daughters back into your ministry. But until then, they won't be taking part." Surprised, Rusty asked why. The man answered, "Because this is legalism. When you tell kids in detail to not step on the lawn, they're going to want to step on the lawn every time. I don't want to become a grandfather when my girls are in high school."

When Rusty asked for more explanation, the dad continued, "It's not about being better at waiting than other people or trying to find the strength on your own to say no, but understanding who we are in Christ. When we keep giving kids rules upon rules, they're going to break them and then punish themselves for being bad, for not meeting the standard we put before them. If they just try harder, they're eventually going to give up because they can't keep up the fight on their own strength. They need to understand who they are in Jesus, understand their identity in Him, understand God's grace, and the fact that, even if they mess up, Jesus still sees them as His masterpiece." (That dad's explanation perfectly described my life for so many years.)

Essentially, the message that came out of the church in the '70s and '80s was a reaction to the "free love" of the '60s. So many student and university ministries started preaching against "sex, drugs, and rock 'n' roll," as in "Here's what we *don't* do as Christians." But the early church we read about in Acts didn't spend time preaching against the culture but spreading the good news of the Gospel to the culture. That's why people came to

Jesus by the thousands when the disciples spoke. Satan wants us to preach about anything or against anything as long as we avoid telling people about Jesus and what His death, burial, and resurrection has provided for us all. I had definitely come out of that era that focused on following rules to try to "keep God happy" with me. And, hard as I tried, that had never worked.

Rusty realized that the father's firm but gentle approach was not to criticize his student ministry but simply explain why he disagreed with the emphasis. That conversation started to take Rusty down a new path. Radically shifting his theology began to create a rift with the staff at the Baptist church where he was serving. People were misunderstanding and misinterpreting his change. He decided the best thing to do to keep peace was to resign and start a new church where he would be the pastor. He would then be free to teach the theology and doctrine he now believed.

This new understanding was essentially what Jesus spent His ministry trying to get across to the Pharisees and Sadducees; the very truth that so many common people, prostitutes, and tax collectors were experiencing when they followed Jesus. In Matthew 9, Mark 2, and Luke 5, the story is told about Jesus responding to the religious leaders' question to the disciples: "Why does your teacher eat with such scum?"

> When Jesus heard this, he said, "Healthy people don't need a doctor—sick people do. Then he added, "Now go and learn the meaning of this Scripture: 'I want you to show mercy, not offer sacrifices.' For I have come to call not those who think they are righteous, but those who know they are sinners." (Matthew 9:12–13 NLT)

So much of modern Western theology has actually been based more on offering sacrifices than showing mercy. Following rules over loving people.

I was soaking all this up like a sponge. It felt like breathing pure oxygen when I'd been suffocating. Even though so much good had come from my counseling, if I were honest, I had never been more unhappy, discontent, and unsatisfied with my spiritual state. But I couldn't figure out why. In 2004 when life began to break down and fall apart, my acquired version of the Gospel was not holding up, because I didn't have the full story. I knew just enough to be dangerous to myself.

On a good day, life seemed great, but then on those days when I was attempting to do all the things that I thought would "get me blessed," when I was "doing it right" and life still fell apart, my response would be "Now, wait a minute, God. I thought I was doing everything You expect of me. Don't I have a high enough score to win Your approval?" What I had always believed was my standing with God was based on *my* behavior. So after feeling like I had been thrown into the fire over and over, my faith didn't have any answers. When you think your relationship with God is based on how well you can toe the line, then when suffering like death and diabetes hit, you have no idea what to do.

My new understanding of the Gospel was what Jesus actually came to offer: the same Gospel that had always been right there in Scripture waiting for me to receive it. For the first time in my life, I understood why Jesus repeatedly said, "Whoever has ears to hear, let them hear" (Mark 4:9). He knew that just because someone speaks does not mean you understand what is being said. I was reading and hearing the Gospel through my own self-made filter, not actually from the Holy Spirit, who came to help us understand and point to Jesus. I was too focused on my failures and shortcomings to look up and see He had already won the victory for me. All I had to do was receive and accept what He had done.

As these truths began to sink in and take hold of my heart, I felt like Luke Skywalker learning to be a Jedi or Batman the first time he put on his utility belt. There were tools and resources I could use on the good days, but *especially* on the bad days. I finally accepted that the Christian life is not about how high my behavior score can be. To explain, God's standard for holiness is always a one hundred. So whether you score a forty or an eighty or even a ninety-nine, you fail. Placing faith in Jesus causes God to see us as one hundred all the time *because* of His Son.

> Yes, Adam's one sin brings condemnation for everyone, but Christ's one act of righteousness brings a right relationship with God and new life for everyone....
>
> So just as sin ruled over all people and brought them to death, now God's wonderful grace rules instead, giving us right standing with God and resulting in eternal life through Jesus Christ our Lord. (Romans 5:18, 21 NLT)

Another important truth I had to learn was how to rest in Christ. That has nothing to do with getting a good night's sleep but with resting my spirit and soul in His grace and mercy. I had to give up the endless battle of trying harder to be good enough. I stopped and waved the white flag of surrender to accept that when I placed my faith in Christ to save me, I received God's approval. This truth was actually true for me, as if Jesus said, "Bart, I've had you all along. I was just waiting for you to give up the fight." Notice how Jesus used the word *rest* twice in this familiar passage:

> Come to me, all you who are weary and burdened, and I will give you **rest**. Take my yoke upon you and learn from me, for I am gentle and humble in heart, and you will find **rest** for your souls. (Matthew 11:28–29)

The only frustration left was asking myself, "This was here for me the whole time, so why didn't I find it sooner?" But thank God I realized the truth when I did. I had the false idea that the Holy Spirit required some kind of dance from me to show up. Discovering and believing He is with me 24-7 was life changing. Today I know that when I walk into any room, anywhere I go, Christ is in me. That changes everything, including my worship and even how I approach worship songs.

I know there are folks who will read these words or hear me talk about this onstage and respond with a warning: "Well, you need to be careful. People may think you're saying that sin doesn't matter. You can go off the rails fast." My response is always the same. No one needs me or anyone else to tell them it's okay to sin. We all sin just fine on our own. The larger truth is, because of Christ, we're going to be okay when we do sin because the cross was enough. None of us needs a license to sin, but we need a remedy when we do. There are at least eighty verses or passages in the New Testament that tell us this truth. Here's one example:

> Day after day every priest stands and performs his religious duties; again and again he offers the same sacrifices, which can never take away sins. But when this priest had offered for all time one sacrifice for sins, he sat down at the right hand of God, and since that time he waits for his enemies to be made his footstool. For by one sacrifice he has made perfect forever those who are being made holy. (Hebrews 10:11–14)

So many Christians fear that if they are set free, they'll become their worst self. But sin has already made us our worst self. We aren't set free *to* sin but *from* sin. If we truly trust what Jesus did for us and that, even when He knows everything we've ever done wrong, He still adores us and is pleased with us, at some point, we start wanting to live for the One who loves us that much. I shouldn't have to remind myself to buy my wife flowers. I should do it because she stuck around and put up with all my nonsense. We live as if we're constantly having to remind ourselves to buy Jesus flowers instead of just telling Him, "I don't understand why you still love me, but because I know you do, I'm so grateful."

Shannon

Rusty's conversations started helping Bart unravel a lot of the legalism and religious concepts from his past, and to understand the true Gospel, the good news that Jesus died, was buried, and resurrected for us. As his journey began, I started noticing changes in Bart. He was approaching life differently. He was showing up more. When a woman starts to see positive changes in her man and asks, "What's happening?" that is nothing but good. When he was home, he was better, which made us all better as he started engaging differently with me and the kids.

As for me, I already felt like I understood God's grace. My parents had modeled it for me when I made mistakes growing up. I believed I had a solid grasp on grace. At first, as Bart and I began to discuss his and Rusty's conversations and he explained his new understanding, I told him, "We grew up in the same church. It wasn't that bad. What are you talking about?" He responded, "But it was just a checklist of what we had to do to be 'good.'" I told him, "Well, I'm the queen of checklists. Give me one and I can nail it. But I'm not feeling the same things you are about our spiritual raising."

One of the key truths that Bart's counseling helped him realize was that he couldn't distinguish between punishment and discipline. To him, his whole life was punishment. Even as a married adult with children, he felt like God was constantly punishing him because he wasn't meeting the standard. With everything that happened to us from 2004 through 2011, Bart's response started to make sense. He had to come to the place to accept truths such as Proverbs 3:11–13: "My child, don't reject the LORD's discipline, and don't be upset when he corrects you. For the LORD corrects those he loves, just as a father corrects a child in whom he delights. Joyful is the person who finds wisdom, the one who gains understanding" (NLT).

We began to see that Bart's upbringing created an attachment to legalistic behavior. Even though we grew up in the same church, we had very different perspectives because of the homes we were raised in and what we were taught, intentionally or unintentionally. As often happens when one spouse goes through a major paradigm shift, for a while, we were on the same path following Jesus, but we were not on the same page in our theology. In those situations, you can't judge each other for not being exactly where the other one is, much like we talked about being in different places with grief. There were definitely a few heated moments during Bart's shift, and I wondered how we would ever realign. As humans have proven over generations, every biblical concept can have its extremes. Yet we always find Jesus right in the middle in perfect balance with the Father.

I had a loving dad who was incredible and always pointed me to Jesus. That was my example. Arthur, Bart's dad, prior to his salvation, was the opposite for him. As Bart got deeper into the Word, he moved to a great place of balance with grace and obedience. Our challenge to each other helped me step out of any legalism I had allowed in my life. In the end, we helped each other grow closer to Jesus, which brought us closer together as a couple.

As Bart and I found our balance individually and together, our motto became "We don't care anymore about what other people think." I grew up as a people pleaser, and Bart grew up hiding everything. His approach was because he felt like if people knew him, they would judge him. For me, I always worked hard to be the best so everyone would be happy with me. We both hit a breaking point to stop caring or worrying about someone judging or hating or disapproving. Discovering God's grace also allowed us to have grace for each other.

Each of us figuring out our identity in Christ gave us a newfound freedom that brought us back to a place of joy and peace. Our decision was not about rebellion against anyone or anything, but rather, making the choice to care the most about what Jesus thinks. Our priorities were made right and put in the right hands. I realized if I'm trying to please people, then I may not please Jesus, which is who I care most about. My obedience to Him can't be filtered through others.

For the past several years, we have taught our kids that navigating friends, relationships, school, and all the stuff of life is tough, but if you know who you are in Jesus, it won't feel quite so hard. That concept has to also be connected to what Jesus talked about in Matthew 11:28–30, a passage Bart previously shared.

My journey in grace was the breakthrough that finally motivated me to not just get *out* of the flower chair but to get *rid* of the flower chair. I began being proactive about my relationship with Shannon and the kids. Even when I was sitting in a depressed state in that flower chair, doing absolutely nothing, when I was at my worst, realizing and receiving the fact that Jesus still loved me literally gave me the strength to get up, get help, and put forth the effort that my family needed. For too long, I was miserable in a comfort zone of my own making. I needed all of our extended family around me to fill in for the fact that I was an absentee dad. With only our family in Nashville, God's work in my heart brought me to the place of saying, "We can do this. Let's go."

To be able to put on the new life in Christ, we have to remove the grave clothes of sin and death. When I made the decision to leave the flower chair for the final time, I left those grave clothes piled up on the cushion, much like Jesus' burial linens that He folded up and left behind in the tomb (see Luke 24:12). This concept is best seen in Paul's words in Romans 6:6–11:

> We know that our old sinful selves were crucified with Christ so that sin might lose its power in our lives. We are no longer slaves to sin. For when we died with Christ we were set free from the power of sin. And since we died with Christ, we know we will also live with him. We are sure of this because Christ was raised from the dead, and he will never die again. Death no longer has any power over him. When he died, he died once to break the power of sin. But now that he lives, he lives for the glory of God. So you also should consider yourselves to be dead to the power of sin and alive to God through Christ Jesus. (NLT)

In the past, Shannon had seen me get excited about something, whether a hobby or some activity, but I would always fizzle out and go back in the chair. I would decide I was going to start exercising to get healthy and lose weight, but before long, give up and go back to the chair. At first, as she started to see me read a book or hear me talk about a Bible verse on grace, I'm sure it just felt like my next fad to her. Like the little boy who cried wolf, I'm sure she thought, *Okay, let's see how long this lasts.*

Also, Shannon had mostly fond memories about her faith in our childhood and teen years. She loved our church and the way we grew up, so she wasn't quick to agree that we had been raised in any legalism. But she eventually came to understand how I translated all that through my shame and guilt from the "everything's my fault" mindset. That's why when she and I would discuss some aspect of this teaching, it wasn't quite the "I've discovered fire" moment for her as it was for me. When she would say, "Bart, I remember our pastor reading those verses and teaching on that," my response was, "Well, then, I must not have been listening because I've *never* heard this." (Once again, "Whoever has ears to hear.")

There were times when Shannon might have been put off a bit with how excited I was. She was thinking, *Whoa, okay, let's ease up, buddy. This may just be your flavor of the month.* But over time, she started to see a very real change taking place in me, which then began to make a major difference in our marriage. Today, she would be the first one to say how much I radically changed. Of course, I still have my moments when some life challenge lands and I want to go back to the flower-chair mindset, but now my foundation—the rock on which my house is built as Jesus taught in Matthew 7—is completely different. I knew I had traded my sand for His rock.

I will forever be grateful to Rusty Kennedy for being available and willing for God to work in and through him to literally change my life as I was coming out of some of my darkest moments. I hope when you get in a bad place, you have a "Rusty" around you. I also hope you will choose to be a "Rusty" to those around you who are struggling.

I knew I had traded my sand for His rock.

Coming full circle in our story and arriving at a new and healthy place, I want to be clear that Shannon has always been the spiritual rock in our family. She was the classic church kid whose parents were Christians. They built the faith house, and she just added her name to the address, so to speak. I feel like we both relied on that faith dynamic for a long time. Her own experience with God brought her to the place of putting her name on her faith, not mine or her parents' or anyone else's. She is constantly seeking truth more than I ever have. Every day for her contains a new discovery as she asks me, "Have you ever noticed what this Scripture says?" to which I often think, *When did you have time to find that?*

In our journey, Shannon has found her voice through gaining spiritual depth out of a commitment to biblical truth. I've never seen her dig in to the Bible more, have more knowledge, and have the ability to apply truth than she does today. Like her dad, she has an engineer's brain that can take in and process a lot of information. She questions everything and seeks truth because she wants to know, not only for the sake of knowing but also because she wants to understand what she believes and why she believes it. Shannon will hear a teaching or someone talk about a verse and she'll ask, "So how does that line up with Scripture?"

Our spiritual journey may have started out in different places, but today we are on the same page and continue to grow closer to the Lord and each other. Throughout our story thus far, we hope you see that, while we had to make some tough choices and commit to some hard work, the real difference in our lives, marriage, and parenting that led us to this point in the story can only be credited to One.

His name is Jesus.

Movie Moment

THE FLOWER CHAIR

In a conversation with the filmmakers, the idea came up that the flower chair was like another character. In the opening scenes, when Movie Sam is young, the chair is visible in the background of the house. At first, it's just part of the room before entering the actual plotline from real life. They wanted to give the chair a fictional backstory that would provide some meaning to why it was in our house at all and offer a reason why I would retreat to that particular chair when life got tough—another "based on a true story" idea.

They created some flashback scenes with legendary actor Dennis Quaid, reprising his role from the first movie as Arthur, my dad, by showing some of the sweet moments between him and Movie Bart after Dad had come to Christ. With no wife, mom, or other females in a house of three bachelors, Arthur comes home with these ugly flower chairs in a feeble attempt to "decorate." But Movie Bart lets

Arthur know they are ugly. Arthur dismisses Bart's criticism and defends his new chairs, creating a funny moment.

Next, in the backstory, we see them sitting in two of the flower chairs that are now outside around a firepit. (Another move only a bachelor would make.) Arthur's health is declining, and he and Movie Bart have a heart-to-heart talk. In real life, there were a number of these types of conversations that happened between Dad and me in his final days. While the setting was totally different, the dialogue was very close.

On the night that scene was shot, I was standing back behind the camera, watching Dennis and John Michael Finley portray Dad and me. As happened many times throughout filming, I was brought to tears again as I watched them having this "life instruction book moment." While Dad is strumming the guitar, like we saw in the original film, father and son are talking, being present with each other. The scene absolutely ripped my heart out. In truth, I don't recall how many moments Dad and I had where I would have been that aware and engaged at only eighteen years old, but regardless, the love shown in the moment was true as well as beautiful. I would have given anything for that scene to have played out exactly that way between me and Dad.

Another fictional scene, back to current day, shows Movie Bart looking for something in storage when he sees the other flower chairs in there. He flashes back to Arthur pulling up with those dumb chairs. In that moment, Movie Bart begins to realize he has to make some big changes as a dad. I liken the scene to Bart's "Rocky Balboa" turning point to stop dying and get busy living.

The incredible production team ended up rebuilding exact replicas of that chair. I remember the first time I saw one on the set, I immediately felt my stomach turn as the sight of it triggered my toxic feelings. When the movie wrapped, they asked if I wanted to take any of the replicas. My answer was clear: "No. Way." I hate that such a long season of my life could be summed up in that stupid chair. If there is a villain in this story, to me, it's that flower chair. But as they are so amazing at accomplishing, the film team created a beautiful moment out of something ugly.

Today in real life, after that chair is long gone, if I'm in a funk, Shannon will ask, "Are you in the flower chair?" It's become a metaphor for when I'm visibly troubled about something. When she uses that reference, I know exactly what she means. Once you've left whatever your "flower chair" is, when life gets challenging and overwhelming, there can be a temptation to go back. As evidence of this very human tendency, where did the resurrected Jesus find Peter after his denial and viewing the empty tomb without yet understanding what had actually taken place? The answer? Right back in his fishing boat, the place where he had last spent a very long and empty night, right before his calling to become a disciple (see John 21).

Chapter 9

BECAUSE HE LIVES

When I was a kid, I spent a lot of time with Mammaw Lindsey, my mom's mom. She was the godliest woman I have ever known. In the first movie, legendary actress Cloris Leachman played my Mammaw Millard. Mammaw was hilarious, just like Cloris portrayed her, and also the person responsible for the band's name. In case you've never heard the story, here it is: On a phone call, Mammaw Millard asked, "Bart, what exactly do you do all day?" I told her, "Well, we're starting a band. All I need to do is come up with a name and I'm good to go." Her response was, "Mercy me, Bart! Why don't you get a real job?!" *No kidding, her exact words.*

In elementary school, most days, I stayed at one of my grandparents' homes until Dad got off work. Whenever I had to spend the night with Mammaw Lindsey, every night she watched the ten o'clock news before bed. When a crime or tragedy was reported, she always responded the same way: by humming softly the hymn "Because He Lives." Every once in a while, she would quietly sing the words to herself. When anything bad happened to me as a child, she would scoop me up in her arms and gently sing that song as only a grandmother who loves Jesus can.

Now, if you were to ask, "So, Bart, is that where you got your voice?" the answer would be "Absolutely not." Mammaw Lindsey could not sing at all. Sometimes, out of frustration, I would ask, "Why are you singing *that* song?" She would always answer, "Jesus is the only thing that makes sense in this world, Bart." That scene played out between us countless times. Growing up, I would make fun of her singing *and* her answer about Jesus. Today, those memories are holy to me.

There are times in life when we feel helpless, maybe even a bit hopeless, and we just need to be reminded, as the chorus tells us, that Jesus makes tomorrow worth facing.

On the morning of 9/11 as Shannon and I were watching the horrible events of that day unfold on live TV, without even realizing what I was doing, I started quietly singing "Because He Lives." In that moment, watching the thick black smoke billow out of the massive towers in New York City, I was not at all aware of what I was doing. After a bit, Shannon asked, "What are you singing?" As I merged back into reality and realized what I had done, her question reminded me of my own to Mammaw Lindsey. I answered, "Oh wow, my grandmother used to sing that hymn all the time when bad news came on TV. I guess my subconscious, or maybe my spirit, knew that was the only response I could have." My grandmother's example had obviously gone down deep and found a place in my soul. When I saw that horrific tragedy, I called up the truth she taught me, just as she had done all those years.

When we first started having to give Sam his shots, he would be so upset and crying. Just like my Mammaw had done with me, I would start softly singing "Because He Lives." Finally, one day when Sam was older, he asked, "Why do you keep singing that song?" His question gave me the chance to tell the story and pass on Mammaw Lindsey's legacy to the next generation. There are times in life when we feel helpless, maybe even a bit hopeless, and we just need to be reminded, as the chorus tells us, that Jesus makes tomorrow worth facing.

Shannon

As Sam entered his teen years and puberty began, his depression continued. I was deeply concerned that his level of despair could be suicidal. He had stopped smiling, rarely said much, and never participated in anything with the other kids. He wanted to be in his room all the time, not doing anything, not wanting to go anywhere, and not talking to anyone. He just wanted to be left alone. At some point, Bart and I told Sam we weren't going to allow him to spend so much time in his room. We knew that isolation can become the enemy's playground, so we told him, "You may be over there in the corner, but you're not going to be alone." So he would sit and play video games more than I ever thought I would allow any kid of mine to do. But at least I could see him—I knew exactly where he was and what he was doing. Still, as time passed, I became more frightened for him.

Our dear friend Rusty, who Bart talked about in the last chapter, was pastoring a church in Indiana, not far from Nashville, and told us he was taking his youth group to camp. He invited Sam to come with them to be around other Christian kids. We trusted Rusty, knew he would take great care of Sam, and would minister to our son. That decision turned out to be a much-needed blessing as everyone there started a beautiful outpouring of love toward him.

Looking for anything we could offer Sam that might be a positive focus, we found out he was interested in photography. We were able to connect him to a well-known photographer in Nashville who, after spending some time with Sam, told us, "I've taught him everything I can. Your son is mastering photography. He's amazing. Now he just needs to keep at it and get better on his own."

Bart also decided to get Sam an acoustic guitar, which turned out to be a great call. Sam spent hours and hours in his room teaching himself to play. We knew that was time well spent because, while the sound was muffled, we could constantly hear him playing and improving. Seeing how serious he was, we arranged for him to take lessons. Through the guitar and photography, Bart and I began to realize when it comes to anything creative, Sam will commit himself and put in the work to become excellent at any craft. Today, if we point to any one thing that saved our son from absolutely crashing in those difficult years, it's the guitar.

After trying to find positive solutions for Sam's depression and isolation, he definitely devoted all his time and energy into learning the guitar.

That instrument became his best friend. From practicing and playing so much, he started to get really good.

When Sam was fourteen, one night I walked by his room and heard him quietly playing *and* singing. As a surprised dad and curious singer, I put my ear to the closed door to try to hear him. After a few minutes, I went and got Shannon. We both sat on the floor outside the door quietly listening. My next move was what all parents attempt to do: capture the moment on my phone. Kneeling down, I hit record on the voice memo app and slowly slid my phone face up under his door, microphone first. I left just enough of the phone sticking out on my side to pull it back through with my fingers. But I obviously wasn't covert enough because, within seconds, he stopped, and the next thing I knew, my phone was sliding across the hallway and banging into the baseboard on the far wall. Sam had kicked it out.

By the time he was fifteen, we allowed Sam to get on Instagram. As we were lying in bed one night, Shannon was holding her phone up in front of her, scrolling through her own account. What I heard next let me know she had tapped on a video of a guy playing and singing. After hearing just a few lines, it grabbed my attention. Thinking how good he was, I said, "Hey, that's pretty awesome. His style is very singer-songwriter. I'd buy that in a heartbeat. Who is it?"

When Shannon didn't answer, I turned my head and looked over to see a tear begin to stream down her face. Choked up, trying to speak, Shannon simply said, "He's your son."

Both of us lay there, listening to Sam's first post—his cover of a Needtobreathe song. We were taking in every word, every note, with the tears rolling. Just our son and his guitar. We had no idea he had gotten to that level as he had been quietly honing his craft all those hours in his bedroom.

Sam

After I gained enough confidence to sing and play entire songs, I started recording myself. Most people who post covers on YouTube or Instagram want you to watch them perform the song as well as hear them. But I was terrified for anyone to see me. So I would hit record on the camera, lay my phone face down beside me, and capture just the audio of me playing and singing. I wasn't ready for anyone to watch me perform yet. (Kind of like the judges' experience on *The Voice*.) When I felt good about a song, I would post it on my Instagram story, just the audio with a black screen. While I wasn't necessarily trying to hide these songs from my family, it took them a while to stumble onto what I was doing.

As a proud dad, I was playing Sam's song for everyone I knew, and saying, "This is Sam! Can you believe it? This is Sam!" I couldn't stop gushing about him. After Brickell heard it, he told me, "Hey, let's get Sam to sing a song some night when we don't have an opening act." I gave him a firm no. When he asked why, I answered, "Because I don't want to be the head coach that gives his kid special treatment and hands him the starting quarterback position." Understanding that my bottom line was actually wanting to protect my son, Brickell let it go and didn't push me.

In 2017, when Sam was almost sixteen, he was out on tour with me. During our set, we would take a short break and a child sponsorship organization would come out and make their presentation. When the talk was done and a volunteer team was passing out packets to anyone in the audience who was interested, I felt like someone should be doing music in the awkward gap of silence. Solving my own concern, I started going out and singing a hymn a cappella. On many nights, my choice was "Because He Lives." Some nights, I would switch and sing a different hymn, but that song was my go-to. Often, I would tell the story about my Mammaw and how I didn't realize how much of an impact hearing her sing the hymn had on me until I was an adult.

One night, I was told, "Hey, we got the song slot covered. You can stay offstage. You don't need to go out and sing." I trusted the decision and didn't ask any questions. Standing in the wings, I looked across the way to see Sam walking out to the mic with his guitar. I was shocked with no idea what was happening.

Here's the rest of the story ...

Sam

Out on the road with Dad, we were in Greensboro, North Carolina, and I was sitting backstage in an empty dressing room before the show. I had my guitar out, noodling around and singing. Immersed in the music, I wasn't paying attention to people walking down the hall.

Mid-song, Brickell walked through the door, larger than life, and in that deep, no-nonsense voice I had heard all my life, he said, "Hey, do you know that song without looking at lyrics or anything?"

Puzzled, I answered, "Yeah, I play it all the time."

He stated, "Good, because you're going out there tonight and playing it for everyone."

As my brain processed what he was saying, adrenaline shot through me. Terrified, I protested, "No! I'm not doing that! I'm not ready to do that!"

Brickell stared at me with his trademark we-ain't-negotiatin' look I had seen him give so many other people over the years, and without changing his tone, he just said, "No, you're going to do it tonight. Get ready." Then, he just turned and left.

I made the assumption that Brickell had talked to Dad. But I found out later he knew nothing about the plan. Brickell had complied with Dad's wishes the year before, but I guess hearing me play and sing that night, having heard enough young artists over the years to believe I was ready, he knew I needed not just a push but a shove onstage.

After telling me I was going to sing, Brickell found the other guys in the band and told them the plan. He also let the crew and soundman know what was about to happen. At the point where everyone left the stage and Dad usually sang the hymn, they told him they were changing things up and got him offstage. From side stage he turned back around to see them bring me in from the other side. There I was with my guitar behind his mic, sweating and shaking and working hard to not pass out from fear.

The song I sang for my first public performance was "Because He Lives."

Starting from my great-grandmother's living room to Dad's a cappella performances and now to me, the timeless hymn was being sung by the third generation. After I finished the song, I didn't acknowledge the crowd or their applause, I just turned and walked off stage. That was *the* biggest feeling of relief I have ever felt in my young life. But in that moment, I realized, *Oh, I'm okay. That wasn't as scary as I thought it would be.* The next night in Johnson City, Tennessee, I begged them to let me sing again.

I found out later that Brickell had talked to Dad the year before about me singing. I heard how he said no because of his concern that, if I wasn't ready, the experience could be traumatic for me. I understood that he was just being a dad first. He had no idea how my first time would go, especially being so young. When Brickell walked in and told me I was singing that night, I was more scared to tell him no than to go onstage and play a song! Giving me no choice was the right choice. Looking back today, I probably wouldn't be where I am in my music career without his push that night. And now, Brickell is my manager too.

Anytime I was out on the road with Dad and heard him sing "Because He Lives," for some reason, the song always caught my attention. Maybe because he sang it a cappella, but to me, the lyrics struck me, being so simple yet so powerful. Because of how I learned the song, I was unknowingly singing it in my own way. I did it in my own style for so long that I actually forgot what the original sounded like. After that night, people would come up to me and say, "I love how you interpret that hymn" or "I love your rendition." I had no idea I had changed it up until Dad explained it to me. Dad started giving me a hard time about having to take that hymn out of his repertoire. He joked that I had taken it away from him.

One of the amazing things about that song is, every time, the whole room is captivated and starts singing with me, which I love. One of the most rewarding moments for an artist is when the crowd sings with you. There's nothing like that feeling of hearing people join you in worship.

Realizing that Sam was onstage singing "Because He Lives" was one of the most unbelievable moments of my life. I was speechless. His performance was so good. After he finished the song and everything had gone great, I decided not to ask Brickell why he didn't tell me. Honestly, I was so glad he didn't. The surprise made the moment much cooler for me. And Sam's decision to sing that song as his live debut was so perfect, especially with our family legacy.

After that first night went so well, we kept Sam out with us and had him sing in that spot instead of me. But a few nights later, he came to me and asked, "Hey, do I have to go out and sing every night?" Surprised, I asked, "What in the world? Why would you not want to do that now? Are you already tired of this? Do you know how long *I've* been doing this every night?" His answer was very sincere: "The rest of the day is so long and boring, just waiting for my four minutes each night."

Honoring Sam's need to be useful, I decided to talk to the child sponsorship group that was traveling with us. I asked, "Hey, do you need any help? My son Sam is tired of waiting around all day to sing. He wants a day job too." They responded, "Absolutely, we'll be glad to find a spot for him." So Sam got a part-time job with them to have more responsibility during the tour day.

But then my son threw me another curveball when he asked, "Dad, do I have to go out and sing tonight? I'd rather keep working with the group than have to stop and go onstage." While I felt like him singing was the real reason he was out with us, I was grateful he was obviously not seeking glory and was showing a strong work ethic. When that tour ended and the next one was scheduled, Sam came to me and asked, "Can I come out to work but not perform?" As a dad, what do you say to that? Of course, I agreed.

Shannon

In our homeschool co-op group, when Sam was sixteen and a sophomore in high school, there was an annual project where each student had to choose an activity that would require them to log forty hours of dedicated time. Then, at the end of the year, each student would make a presentation of their work to the student body.

At first, Sam was stumped and struggled with what to do. As he talked it over with us, Bart offered, "Hey, Sam, because you've started singing and playing, why don't you try writing a song? I can guide you through the process." After that conversation, I told Bart, "I'm not sure this is going to work. Sam has never written a song. That's your thing, not his. Maybe you need to help him figure out what *he* wants." Bart responded, "But songwriting's the only thing I really know how to do to help him with a project like this." A little scared and a bit hesitant, mostly out of desperation, Sam agreed.

We already knew he could play and sing, but we had no idea if he could write a song. As Sam was getting started, Bart told me, "I'm praying this is good, because I don't want to have to tell him if it's not!" As Sam started logging his hours, he soon came back with some lyrics for him and Bart to begin work on a melody to flow with the words. Once they felt like they had arrived at a complete song, they went to Tim Timmons to ask if he would help record it in his basement studio.

At the private Christian school where our co-op met for this project, Sam was too terrified to sing the song live on his guitar. So he played the recording for the student body at school through the PA system. When the song ended, the whole room went crazy. His friends were saying, "Sam! What a great song!"

In the music business, it's called a triple threat when you can sing, play, and write. Little did we know all these elements were going to come together for Sam to create a career.

For Christmas that year, Shannon and I gave Sam studio time with Ben Shive to record his version of "Because He Lives." (Ben has worked with many artists, such as Colony House, JJ Heller, and Ellie Holcomb.) I told Ben I wanted Sam to be able to explore the song on his own without being in my shadow and, whatever happened, good or bad, to just run with it. I wanted Sam to be free to share his opinions and take the song wherever he thought it should go. When they were trying to finish up, there were some high harmony parts that Sam wanted. He asked Ben, "Do you think my dad would come and do these background vocals?" Ben assured him I would.

At the studio with me in the vocal booth, I could see Sam and Ben talking and grinning. Ben told me later how he was explaining to Sam, "Your dad doesn't know what to do with you. But he's doing everything to try to get me to bring the right stuff out of you. You have access to him like no one else does, so you need to take full advantage of your opportunity." Ben built me up to Sam as a dad, singer, and songwriter, which was so kind and amazing of him to do.

That day in the studio turned out to be a major turning point for our relationship. In fact, Sam told Ben I was the only reason he was into music. If you have ever parented a teenager, then you know most of them think that whatever their parents do, they can't possibly know what they're talking about. After the experience of helping Sam write his first song and Ben's pep talk, music became our connecting point. To this day, Sam respects everything I say about music and wants my opinion above anyone's. Whenever he finishes a new song, the first people he plays it for are Shannon and me.

Shannon

After Sam graduated from high school, he was accepted into a pilot program at Lipscomb University in Nashville for kids who want to be artists or musicians. The goal was to expose them to songwriting, touring, and the business aspect of the music industry. As a two-year program, it would be much like a hands-on technical school inside the university. The terrifying challenge for us was that they required students to live on campus. This would be Sam's first time completely on his own in managing his disease. My mother's-heart was telling me, "He's already not taking care of himself very well with us, and now we're going to let him go live in a dorm with roommates?! With no one to watch over him, we could lose our son." That thought created pure fear for me. The reality that parents of type 1 diabetic kids know is they can have a severe blood sugar drop in their sleep and not wake up. They go into a coma and die.

Meeting Sam's three roommates, I found out one of the guys had a sister who was diabetic. I talked to him and asked, "If you hear Sam's alarm at night and he doesn't wake up, would you please wake him up for me?" Being a kid himself with the best of intentions, he answered, "Oh, sure, Mrs. Millard. I can help." To no surprise in a roomful of four university freshmen guys who all think they're bulletproof at that age, I found out later that none of that was happening. While I wanted to ask, "Why would you not help your friend?" my rational self said, "Shannon, you're asking way too much and trying to control too much. Even though it's really hard, you have to give this to the Lord."

I cried lots of tears during that very long semester. When I let go the first time, things did not go well, so anything close to that feeling created a trigger for me. With no apologies, we were definitely "helicopter parenting" him with the only goal of keeping our son alive. We were most certainly reacting out of trauma. I can tell anyone all the right things that should have been done, but I just couldn't bring myself to do anything differently.

For all the moms out there, surrendering our parenting to the Lord will always be the best thing to do, but that does not mean it will be easy. When you have a two-year-old with type 1 diabetes, you can't possibly know how he or she is going to turn out after a childhood of getting so much attention, even negative attention. But today, thank God, I see this beautiful young man who has a deep heart of compassion.

Sam ended up being at Lipscomb for just one semester because, like me, he decided to leave to start going on the road with us. But that four months ended up being the best thing for him because he got a taste of real freedom and had an opportunity to grow in his independence that we all knew needed to happen.

For the next two MercyMe tours, Sam went out with us to work full-time and not sing. To be fair, the one venue he did ask to go out and perform at was the legendary Red Rocks Amphitheatre in Colorado. To this day, I cry when I hear Sam sing. *Every* time. The tears are from being proud of my son and thanking God that he loves Jesus and is healthy.

The tears are also because I love his voice that much, the voice of that diabetic kid I thought I had ruined.

Quite often, I remember Billy Graham's prayer for Sam—that God would either heal him or use him with his condition to change the world.

So far, the answer is to change the world.

Movie Moment

BLOOD BROTHERS

Having been heavily invested in two movies about my life, I've learned a lot about the process of trying to get years of a story crammed into less than two hours. Everyone from the writers to the producers to the director has to find the most creative ways to communicate specific dynamics in a very short span to the audience. Creating scenes in a movie is a lot like writing a song. I have three and a half minutes to capture the essence of a major dynamic in my life. If I tried to tell the entire story, one song would become a musical, so I have to find a way to communicate the concept so that the listener understands and relates the lyrics to their own lives.

Especially when there is a lot of tragedy in a film, you have to figure out how to interject some lighthearted moments or comic relief. In *I Can Only Imagine 2*, the guys in the band made for an easy way to provide that element, because humor has always been an everyday part of our lives on the road. You can't stay sane out there without creating some fun. So the actors who played Movie Mike, Nathan, Robby, and Barry become the "crazy uncles" to Movie Sam because, being real, Movie Bart is just not funny, especially around his son.

Years ago, there was a real-life moment when Sam was out on the road with us and had to check his blood sugar. The guys were freaking out over the thought of having to give yourself a shot. I told them, "The shot's nothing compared to the finger prick. I hate the finger prick." They came back, "Are you kidding?" I reminded them how I had to learn to give a shot on an orange and then move up to giving myself an empty shot because the nurses wanted Shannon and me to know how it felt. That led to me convincing all the guys to prick their fingers. Based on their reactions to pain and blood, to no surprise, they were a bunch of wimps. A couple of them couldn't do it.

In the film, a fictional scene was shot where the band bus breaks down on the side of the road with Sam and our friend Tim Timmons on board. They make this little firepit and get out their lawn chairs to sit while waiting on a mechanic. The discussion becomes "What's your biggest fear?" prompting everyone to start talking about their various phobias. When they get to Sam, his answer is needles. Tim is surprised and asks, "What are you talking about? You've had to deal with a ton of needles." Sam responds, "Yeah, but I still hate them."

That's when the decision is made for everyone to stick their fingers. Gathered around the firepit, everyone gets one of Sam's finger prick needles. They all count down and draw blood. Being on the same side of this moment, Movie Sam and Movie Bart are laughing at them all, creating a connection for the two of them. Then, Movie Nathan says, "Blood brothers, what say ye?" as he holds his thumb proudly up and outward. The other guys smile and answer, "I'm in!" The scene depicts a very real solidarity, communicating to Sam, "We're in this with you."

I was on the set that night and watched this scene play out. Once again, I couldn't hold back my tears. Because the truth is, we *are* brothers and that scene in the movie does represent what those guys are willing to do and what they have meant to Sam his entire life.

As for the real Bart, I'm all about having fun and being funny! I don't keep a conversation serious for very long. Sometimes that's a deflection, but it's also just me and who I am. The interesting thing about both these films is I come off very serious and intense for most of the scenes because the content in these movies deals with the worst parts of my life. They couldn't be a comedy, because what happened in real life is not funny at all.

When I consider that dynamic, I often think about Robin Williams. He was one of the funniest, most creative comics in history, but he was always trying to cover up what was going on inside him. Such a tragic irony that a man that funny would kill himself. But most comedians will admit they have some sort of pain or insecurity they are trying to hide or compensate for. My imagination and sense of humor were always used for exactly that reason.

I have joked that this book should be titled *Part-Time Job*, not "job" like work, but Job, the man in the Old Testament. While I'm certainly no Job, I do understand much more than I'd like to admit about how he must have felt dealing with such loss and tragedy, lying there wondering where God was. That said, while most of the story is very serious and intense, in the end, because of that same God, Job was the one laughing.

But even if You don't
My hope is You alone

Life with Chris

Type 1 diagnosis

Happier times

Beach fun

Christmas!

Happy New Year!

Sam and his guitar

Family time!

Claudette and Frank

CHLOE & SAM

Chloe and Sam

I Can Only Imagine premiere day

Chapter 10

FATHERS AND SONS

Getting plugged into life in Nashville, I joined a Christian men's group where all the guys were either artists or pro athletes—current and retired. At one meeting, the opening question was "What was the relationship with your dad like?" I was sitting there thinking that no one was going to be able to top my story. But then Barry Zito, a fourteen-year veteran major league pitcher who had moved to Nashville after leaving baseball, started to share. He talked about how his dad, who had passed just a few years before, had been his best friend in the whole world. He had been there at every single game since Little League. As a major leaguer, he either saw his dad or talked on the phone with him daily, whether playing home games or on the road. After sharing how great his dad was, Barry ended with "I've spent thousands of dollars in counseling trying to get out from under his shadow, to try and figure out who I am on my own and be half the man he was." (Barry told the entire story in his book *Curveball.*)

As I sat there riveted to Barry's confession, I was thinking, *I spent thousands of dollars in counseling because my dad belittled and beat me!* In that moment, the truth hit me that, whether amazing or abusive, a son has to find his own identity outside of his father. If a son grows up idolizing his dad, thinking he can do no wrong, then the battle becomes, like Barry said, "I'll never be half the man he was." That resignation for a young man can lead to extremes of an unhealthy drive for success or giving up, which can then create responses like medication and addiction. Ironically, if a son despises his father, the same two extreme outcomes can take place. The best or the worst relationship can take us to an unhealthy place as men. After counseling and opening up to the guys in that group, I started to realize, as men, we are all in the same boat more than we want to admit because, whether dads or not, we are all someone's son.

After my father came to Jesus, through our discussions and reconciliation, I learned that he felt like he couldn't get fatherhood right. That's why, out of frustration and guilt, he decided to act like he didn't care about me. And I assumed by his behavior that he actually didn't. I couldn't see the motive, only the clear message sent. In the years after Mom left before he got sick, Dad had fully committed to the attitude of *Why bother?* After I became a father myself, I realized how easy it is for difficult circumstances outside your control to break you as a man.

Compared to my father, I felt like I was in the opposite place. I loved Sam so much, but because I had decided to give in to my inability to "fix" the diabetes, while struggling with so much grief and guilt, the result ended up repeating in the next generation. Sam made the same assumption I had in my teen years: Dad must not care. I ended up succumbing to *Why bother?* which put me in the flower chair. Sam couldn't see the motive either, only the clear message I sent.

Sam

My first memory of realizing my life wasn't normal because of the diabetes was when I was in third grade. A magazine wanted to publish an article on Dad through the lens of having a child with type 1 diabetes. The writer and photographer came to our house to document a normal day of navigating my care. They took pictures of me getting my blood sugar tested, receiving shots, and counting out the carbs I was eating. I didn't understand what the big deal was and why they were interested in what I thought was normal, standard procedure stuff.

But when the magazine article came out, for the first time I saw my life as *abnormal* compared to other kids. I felt like the guest of honor at a pity party. I had never actually connected the dots that my friends didn't have to do what I did. I'd never had to think about the difference before because no one had ever pointed it out to me. That was the shift where I saw my life from someone else's perspective.

As I got older and learned more about the kind of childhood and upbringing Dad had come from, I started to see how and why he processed my disease the way he did. I realized all the ways he was beating himself up and how he was so determined to not turn out like his father. The fear and guilt brought him to the point that he couldn't and wouldn't deal with the reality of my disease. For a while, I was angry that he wouldn't open up and talk about how he felt around me. One of the revelations I heard for the first time came during the process of making the *Imagine* movie. I heard Dad say he realized as a kid how he would rather get negative attention from his father than no attention at all, after having to deal with his dad acting like he didn't care.

In a strange way, Dad's confession brought some understanding to how I felt with him. I went through a season where I would rather him get mad and yell at me than have to wonder if he cared or not. Oddly, at the same time, deep down, I never questioned that he loved me. Even after I had learned the entire story, I never thought he turned out like his dad, how Arthur was before he came to Christ. But I do recall at one point telling Dad, "This is me and you! We are not you and your father! I want a dad that I *know* cares about me."

For Mom and me, we have always been much more confrontational in our relationship. We want to get everything out on the table, even if the process is hard at the time. From Dad being gone and removing himself while at home, he and I had distance in our relationship. As I got older, I could see that affected our circumstances, like when he wasn't clued in on the most recent information and treatment of my diabetes because of being on the road.

As the kids of all the members of MercyMe started to get old enough to go out on the road with our dads, we would jockey for an open spot, a bunk on the bus on a tour weekend. Our dads may have been going to work, but for us, those days were a vacation. When I was around fifteen, I stopped wanting to go out on tour with him. I started to feel like I was in the way, not a kid anymore just wanting to have fun. For example, I would be sitting on a road case watching the stage setup and a crew guy would walk up and say, "Hey, kid, I need you to move. I have to get in there." Someone nearby would tell him, in front of me, "Hey, be careful. Don't mess with him. That's Bart's kid." The last thing I wanted was attention or any kind of special treatment. While I'm sure a lot of artists' kids love getting treated like some kind of royalty, I hated that dynamic. I struggle with attention anyway, but particularly negative attention.

Finally, I decided if I was going to go out on the road again, I had to have a purpose. I needed a job, a reason to be out there. Voicing that desire to Dad led to me working with some of the nonprofits that go out on tours to promote their ministry. For a while, I worked for Mark Stuart, the former lead singer for Audio Adrenaline, who is a big part of MercyMe's history. Ironically, that decision is actually what led to me being in the dressing room where Brickell heard me play and sing.

After that performance of "Because He Lives" in 2017, because so many concertgoers watch the entire show through their phone cameras while they video, people posted clips of me singing on social media and YouTube. I could tell a lot of them had no idea who I was. But many of the ones who figured it out posted captions like "This is Bart Millard's son" or "Bart's kid who has diabetes" or "the kid who was the reason behind some of MercyMe's songs."

Scrolling through those posts, I felt like I didn't have a name and certainly didn't have my own identity. A lot of the core MercyMe fans had heard Dad tell our family's story. The problem was, I was being labeled by diabetes. Of course, I understood why people were making that connection, but I'll be honest: None of that sat well with me. Nobody wants to only be known for a health issue that's just one aspect of who they are. I wanted to be known for who *I* am, not for a disease or my dad or even a song. After that, I became determined to bring something to the table myself—something all my own.

After counseling and my grace transformation, I began to see the fruit of working hard to rise up out of the ashes of my past. But I also started to realize there was a strong chance that Sam would be sitting in a counselor's chair one day, trying to deal with the baggage he inherited from me. As parents, dads or moms, so many of us try to "fix" the pain we came out of to try and save our kids from experiencing the same thing. We attempt to avoid recreating our childhood in our kids. But then we can overcompensate and swing the pendulum to the other side of the issue, which is why, especially in our American culture, you often hear, "I grew up with nothing, so I vowed that my kids wouldn't want for anything" or "My dad ruled the house with an iron fist, so I'm going to allow my kids the freedom I never had."

Unfortunately, as sinners raising sinners, we can create an entirely new set of issues for the next generation. The very thing we are determined to avoid still happens. We can cause our kids pain even after taking a completely different approach. Honestly, when someone says, "Oh, that family is so dysfunctional," the truth is, all families are in some way. The mess just looks different, depending on the core problems.

When I was growing up, my dad, my older brother, and I never had anything. We were always broke. Because God chose to bless me with success right as I was becoming a father, I'm grateful that cycle could end with me. Being a good provider has always been a major priority for me. My primary way of showing my kids I care has been to have the best possible place for them to live and make sure all their material needs are met. Because my life always felt so uncertain and insecure, my goal was to make sure my kids never experienced those feelings. Yet I can admit today that I placed too much focus on that provision, far more than I should have. Just because we can doesn't always mean we should. The apostle Paul addressed that issue in 1 Corinthians 10:23: "You say, 'I am allowed to do anything'—but not everything is good for you. You say, 'I am allowed to do anything'—but not everything is beneficial" (NLT).

After counseling and my grace transformation, I began to see the fruit of working hard to rise up out of the ashes of my past.

Another way I worked hard to counter my upbringing was to be sure to tell my kids I love them. But real communication in talking one-on-one was never my strong point. By the time our oldest kids started coming into their preteen and teenage years, my ever-present, in-house voice of accusation in my head would whisper, "They don't want you around because you're really a dork." (Yes, "dork" was the usual diss of myself.) Yet, if most dads are honest, we figure out down the road that our kids would rather have had focused time with us than another toy, game, or device. Often, Shannon would tell me, "Bart, you need to lean in and ask them what's going on in their lives." But when a man has never been good at that with *anyone*, and the voice in your head is telling you they don't want you around, that accusation becomes a huge hurdle, if not a wall you hit. I don't offer that as an excuse but a reality of what far too many dads feel, as well as fight.

Sam

For most of my years growing up, I just saw Dad as my dad. What he does or is known for in Christian music was not really something we were aware of as kids. Years ago, the guys in MercyMe created a private channel where they posted family videos for archives. There're around five hundred there of all the band kids. Some of my best childhood memories of my dad are on those videos that involved me, Gracie, and Charlie. Dad would put a sock on his hand, calling the character Johnny Socksniffer. He would hide out of the camera view and use the puppet to interview us kids. We were the guests and Johnny was the host. We all thought he was so fun and funny. Occasionally, when we pull up those videos to watch as a family, I am very thankful we have such great memories.

Another popular "remember the time when" family story happened when I was four or five years old. My dad, my uncle, and I were going to a Rangers ball game and we got stuck in Dallas traffic. With nowhere to go, I told Dad I had to pee really bad. The only thing we had in the car that might work was an empty Coke can. Because we were barely moving, Dad handed me the can and told me to "go" in there. Well, there's not a whole lot of room in those small tab openings. As soon as I started "going," of course, I couldn't possibly aim and missed the hole. Immediately, pee began to hit the can top and deflect and spray all over the car, all over Dad and my uncle. They were both yelling, "Sam, stop! Stop!" *But when you gotta go, you gotta go, right?*

Dad didn't talk about his career much until I got older and became interested in his line of work. I didn't start to realize the weight of some of his accomplishments until the first movie came out. I just hadn't understood what a big deal "Imagine" was as a song. Once I realized how popular the band had become, I started struggling with not wanting to ride Dad's coattails, like the whole "nepo baby" thing that came out several years back about the kids of Hollywood actors. Same principle, as in "Oh, you only got here because of your dad or mom." When I decided that I genuinely wanted to stake my claim in Christian music and knew this is what I felt led and called to do, I realized I would have to set myself apart. I couldn't get very far just being known as Bart's son.

My dad and I being in the same music genre created an uphill battle for me as a singer, songwriter, and artist, especially when it also happens to be one of the smallest in the music industry. For a short time, that's part of why I completely pushed Christian music away. Not my faith, just the genre. But I got too caught up in how artists get pigeonholed rather than just focusing on writing what comes out of my own voice and creativity. Ironically, at the same time, I was leading worship anywhere I could. That was my only outlet to do music. When I began to feel like I was going in circles, I decided to come full circle and focus back where I began, on songs like "Because He Lives."

When Sam was invited to lead worship at a nearby youth camp with about fifty kids, I went and sat in the back. I thought about how I was around his age the first time I led worship at a camp. At the time, I had no idea where my life was headed. No clue what was coming. Sitting there listening to my son, I could see how he had his entire life ahead of him. I saw how carefree he was and how he loved being in the moment with the music. Like me back then, if he messed up, he just laughed it off and kept going. He knows he has so much to learn, so he's willing to listen to me, which creates such a great relationship for us today.

A lot of kids want nothing to do with whatever their dad does. In my case, the children of artists often want to distance themselves from what took their dad away from them all the time. That's why I can get emotional when I think about the fact that Sam wants to be a part of the same industry, even the same genre as me. Someway, somehow, he got something out of all those years. To be able to know your kid cares about what you do is an incredible feeling. To this day, I know if I say something boneheaded, he's tempted to think I'm just some old guy, but when it comes to music, we have a mutual respect. I love how much Sam loves music, to the point where he's willing to sacrifice to do it. I was the same way back in the early days of MercyMe. For someone to make it in this industry, they have to be able to love it so much that they won't walk away when times get tough. And, especially today, it gets difficult for everyone at some point. But Sam loves music that much.

Sam

In the spring of 2022, when I was twenty years old, I was on tour with Dad. We were supposed to fly nonstop from LA to Nashville, but the flight got delayed. The airline switched us to go from LA to Denver, then Denver to Nashville. Right after we got off the plane in the Mile High City, my blood sugar suddenly dropped. There wasn't enough time for me to grab something to eat because we were so tight on the flight schedule.

As everyone was running down the concourse, every man for himself, I started to feel lightheaded and thought, *Great, I'm going to pass out*. Trying to walk quickly on the moving sidewalk, I fell face-first, out cold. Coming in and out of consciousness, all I saw were total strangers bent down, trying to help me. No one I knew. That particular day, my numbers hadn't been very low. That's the toughest part about type 1—you never know when a sudden drop can occur. It just happens. Then you can overcorrect and go too high. That's the unpredictable part of this disease that can cause you to live in fear.

I have no idea who or how, but someone finally realized I didn't make it to the gate and they backtracked to find me. When I woke up in the hospital, there was Dad. Right away, I could tell he was clearly freaked out. He was beating himself up that he didn't stay with me and wasn't there when I fell. This was the first time I had woken up in an ER to see Dad by himself next to the bed. Before, it had been Mom. When he saw I was awake, he immediately began saying, "It's going to be okay. You're all right." He was very reassuring. Dad was typically calm, so seeing him that worried but also nurturing really stuck with me.

When I realized what had happened and that we were in a hospital in Denver, I began to freak out too, concerned that Dad could miss the next show. As soon as he realized my fear, he assured me, "That doesn't even matter. I'll cancel the next show ... I'll cancel the rest of the tour if we have to. The priority right now is what's happening with you." Later that day, my numbers came up and stabilized, and I was well enough to be released to fly home with Dad.

That day in the hospital, seeing and hearing him put me first, even ahead of his career, was the biggest moment I recall for him and me. With Mom not there, Dad definitely stepped up. Out of another bad situation in our family, God brought a great deal of good.

Shannon

A brand-new dynamic was introduced into our lives when we decided to go on a vacation with Rusty and his family. By the end of the week, we all could clearly see that something was beginning to bud between Sam and their daughter, Chloe. We saw two teenagers look at each other differently. I remember asking Bart, "Do you see that? Something's funny. That's interesting, but actually very cool." Sam discovered he was able to confide in Chloe in a way he never had with anyone else. He would spill his guts to her for hours. For the next several years, Chloe was able to walk with Sam emotionally and spiritually through our difficult move and transition.

Sam and Chloe started "going together" when they were around thirteen. Over the years, they broke up and got back together two or three times. When Sam was seventeen, Chloe broke up with him again. I remember he was sobbing, and I had never seen him like that. Especially as a teenager, he typically appeared like he had it all together. Sam pulled me aside and basically asked, "Dad, can you help me with how to deal with this? Could we just sit and talk?"

Having my daughters ask me something like that was one thing, but for Sam, who is very quiet and private like I am, that moment was a major breakthrough. That was the first time he had ever said anything like that, essentially saying, "I just need you to show me how to deal with this. Tell me what I'm supposed to do. How can I get through this? I need you to talk to me, Dad." We ended up sitting on his bed for the next two or three hours that night, navigating our way through heartbreak. I was able to tell him about me and Shannon, how we broke up a few times, and how hard that was. Especially not knowing at that point if they would get back together, I had to be honest that this was going to hurt really bad. And how only time can heal.

Sam and I always joked around and made each other laugh, but we had never had a heart-to-heart like that. So much of our time had been consumed with "Is your blood sugar high or low?" That became such a constant part of life that us just talking got set aside and overshadowed. In fact, his condition caused me to be around him far more than all the other kids. I'm sure they would say, "All you did was hang out with Sam." While I would completely understand their perspective, in reality, all we did was deal with his diabetes. Our first real conversation happened that night and took our relationship to a new and different place. That was the beginning of us agreeing that I was going to check in with him once a week about life, not diabetes.

The thing I love most about Sam as an artist is that he doesn't like to self-promote, especially on social media. He makes me want to root for him because he doesn't have what I call "the hustle muscle" in him. I think he gets that from Shannon. Neither of them are "look at me" people. Shannon would much rather do what she loves and take a step back. Sam has followed her lead. Also like their mom, Sam and Sophie are "old souls" who have what we call the "justice gene." There's a deep loyalty, but also a sense that when something is not right, it hurts their hearts.

When everything first began connecting for Sam with his music, the next thing I was waiting on was for his love for Jesus to blossom. That can't be taught; it has to be caught. He had to find his faith for himself, to call his own. I didn't want my son's belief to be like the eighth-grade science project that your parents build and let you put your name on. As far as I know, there's been no Damascus-road moment for Sam. But hearing the music he's writing tells me his love for the Lord is at a solid place. He's also realized he can do Christian music the way he wants to do it, not the way I have, or the way Christian radio or anyone else tells him to do it. He's also finding out how his own music can be a vehicle to express how he feels about being a diabetic. But that is all part of what's giving him his voice. He's been given something to say to a generation that doesn't want to be alone and wants to feel like they are accepted. Exactly the heart of the Gospel.

As a dad who's a sinner saved by grace raising a son who's also a sinner saved by grace, our primary connecting point is the truth we discovered for ourselves in Malachi 4:6:

> He will turn the hearts of the fathers back to their children and the hearts of the children to their fathers. (NASB)

Movie Moment

GRANDFATHER'S GUITAR

In the film, when Movie Bart is going through storage, after he finds the other flower chairs, he also sees Arthur's acoustic guitar. Obviously, Bart doesn't play guitar. That's when he remembers that his dad wanted him to give his guitar to somebody who could play and appreciate it. Arthur says, "A guitar just sitting and not being played is like a boat in the desert." When Movie Bart sees the guitar, his expression lets you know he's thinking, *I have to give this to Sam!* The guitar is then passed on to Arthur's grandson, the next generation.

Here's the real-life story that inspired the movie scene: Shannon's dad, Frank, had an old Gibson big-body guitar that he had played throughout her childhood. For years, he had always told Sam, "When I'm gone, I want you to have this." After we moved to Nashville, anytime Sam went back to visit family in Greenville, he would play that beautiful guitar. Not long before Frank passed away in late 2024, he told Sam, "Why in the world am I waiting? Why would I want to be gone before you get this? I want to be the one to give it to you. And I want you to lead people to Jesus with this guitar."

Frank was so proud to give his beloved guitar to his grandson. Today, that guitar is being played for the exact reason he wanted—to share the good news.

Chapter 11

ANOTHER DAY, ANOTHER *X*

In *I Can Only Imagine 2*, Milo Ventimiglia plays Tim Timmons. Tim will never let me live down the fact that the dad in the hugely popular TV show *This Is Us* was cast to play him. In this chapter, I want to tell you the story of my relationship to Tim, his mentorship of Sam, and our family's connection to his family.

In February of 2013, MercyMe was headlining the Rock and Worship Roadshow tour with Jeremy Camp and seven other Christian artists. It's common practice with that many artists for the tour manager to call everyone together before the buses and semis roll out for the first time to go over the rules, protocols, and schedules. With so many people, any disorganization can cause life to get chaotic quickly. (Brickell has always described dealing with the organization of musicians and creatives this way: "It's like trying to herd cats.")

On the first day of tour, as all the artists, bands, and crew members began showing up, introducing themselves, and catching up with friends, this complete stranger walked right past everyone else, came straight up to me, and with a big smile, confidently stated, "Hey, I've been told I'm supposed to be your new best friend." (You've been with me long enough in these pages to already know that was not the right approach if you even remotely want to be my friend.) From his opening line, I knew there was no need to try to rack my brain for how I might know this guy. I had no clue who he was—if he was an artist, someone's band member, or from the crew. With his shaved head, thick beard, and big black glasses, he looked more like a genius at the Apple store.

Completely thrown, with a touch of sarcasm mixed with skepticism, I gave him the best comeback I could think of: "Oh, yeah?" Grinning from ear to ear, he responded, "Yeah, the guys from The Afters told me, 'You and Bart are going to love each other.'" (The Afters were a Christian band we knew from the Dallas area.) He stuck out his hand and announced, "I'm Tim Timmons!"

I half-heartedly shook his hand and said, "I'm Bart ... You have to be messing with me, right? There's no way your name is really Tim Timmons."

With his huge smile breaking into a laugh, he responded, "No, that is my real name."

What Tim said next surprised me even more. "I heard you've joined the revolution about God's grace and identity in Christ."

I had to assume the guys in The Afters must have told him, which is why they encouraged Tim to meet me. But regardless, he was absolutely right. As we started this tour, I was in the middle of my new journey.

After asking around about the mysterious "Tim Timmons" from folks on the tour, I found out he was a singer-songwriter newly signed with Reunion Records. His first album called *Cast My Cares* was coming out in four months with a June release date. The label had arranged for him to have one of the opening slots as a "lights-up act," meaning the venue house lights are all on and you play your set right after the doors open. Those slots are not for the faint of heart, because people are walking in, talking to ushers to try to find their seats, and visiting with their friends. Very few people are actually paying attention, much less listening. Even singing a worship song for a Christian audience, it can feel like you're just background music at a party. Because Tim was so new and his album wasn't out yet, not many folks, including most of us on the tour, knew anything about him.

As the days passed and I was around Tim more, I can tell you that he comes with some shock value. The orientation experience is very different from getting to know most people. But I have to confess that his intro line to me turned out to be absolutely right. The grace awakening that had rocked my world had rocked his as well. We were on the same page in a refreshed, reset relationship with Jesus. That connection and his quirky, clever humor caused Tim and me to quickly hit it off. (I was as surprised as anyone.) Like concentric circles, there was a lot of opposite between us, yet just enough overlap to make it interesting and intriguing. I would describe Tim as infectious. (Not infection ... infectious.) He has an inspirational, contagious joy about him that, particularly for an introvert like me, can be overwhelming. I've always been suspicious of people like that, as in, "There's no way you can be happy all the time. This has to be a put-on." Yet from day one of meeting Tim to the last time I saw him, that's just who he is. He's the real deal.

More often than not, I would be irritated and distance myself from someone with Tim's personality, but he is never annoying to me. No question, though, that his energy level is like the legendary scene in the parody movie *Spinal Tap* where the guitarist says most rock bands' amps go to ten, but theirs goes to eleven. That's Tim—turned up to eleven. I just assumed after we met that first time he would dial it back a bit, but he never did. He reminds me of a really sweet and loyal puppy who's always happy and excited to see you.

At times, Tim's humor could be uncomfortable and even embarrass me. To give you an example of the kind of situation that would frequently take place, one time we were sitting in a car in a parking lot having a very serious and deep talk when these two ladies walked up to their car parked next to ours. For some strange reason—and I'm not making this up—one woman was carrying a milkshake machine with the big silver cup. The other had a vacuum cleaner. I have no idea why, but that was the scene. Distracted by two people carrying such random items, that was just too much for Tim to ignore. There was no way he was going to let this opportunity pass him by, *especially* with me.

As they approached their car, Tim rolled his window down and asked, "Ma'am, am I picking up the milkshake machine or the vacuum? I didn't understand which one in your text." Both ladies stopped in their tracks and turned to look at us with very stern, borderline-offended expressions. Immediately, I cringed and wanted to disappear. They clearly didn't think the question was funny. I thought, *This is it. We're about to be impaled by a vacuum cleaner as the windshield gets smashed by a milkshake machine.* I absolutely hate when someone inserts themselves into an uninvited situation when you have zero idea what might happen next. And Tim knows that.

With the ladies staring at him not knowing how to respond, Tim broke out his joyful grin, which then absolutely defused any possible offense. That's when he and the appliance ladies burst out laughing. My embarrassment turned to shock when I saw them completely change their response. After

Tim said, "Have a great day!" and they had stowed their appliances in the trunk and driven away, I told him, "Would you *please* stop doing that stuff with me around?! Just stop it, man! We were in the middle of a serious talk. I don't even remember what I was saying now!" In situations where I would get beat up, Tim will make a new friend.

But if you are going to hang with Tim Timmons, you'd better get used to it and accept his view of reality, because he does that kind of thing all the time. In fact, he looks for opportunities. It's everything I wouldn't do and everything I couldn't do. Yet, oddly, that was something I came to love about him because I *don't* have the nerve or the guts to try that. To Tim, there is no such thing as a stranger. He puts people into two categories: those he knows and those he hasn't met yet. One thing is for sure—he is not afraid to walk up and talk to anybody. After witnessing several of those random encounters, I asked him, "How have you *not* ever been punched in the face? Why do people always laugh when you do those things?" Now, in reality, because I have made how I feel very clear to Tim, he intentionally does it all the time with the singular goal of making me uncomfortable. Even squirm, if at all possible.

Another time Tim saw someone who had been to Cancún or some beach town where tourists get the tiny, tight beads woven into their hair. (A decision I bet most people quickly regret.) Tim walked up and said, "Wow, I was going to get those exact same beads!" (Remember, I told you he has a completely bald, shaved head.) I sighed, closed my eyes, and waited for the angry outburst. But was this complete stranger upset or angry? No! The person broke out a big smile and responded, "Oh, you so should have! ... The pink ones!" Then they both laughed together, like they had known each other since college. Somehow, beyond my reasoning, Tim can bring joy to complete strangers. His good heart, coupled with a lack of fear, absolutely draws me to his personality and amazing ability to interact with anyone.

No surprise then that Tim is also known for being a big hugger. Okay, actually "hug" is not a strong enough word. Tim *embraces* people. Countless times, I have seen him bear-hug someone, never inappropriately but out of a genuine love for people. But when he introduced himself to me, Tim had evidently gathered enough intel to know to give me some space, some time to get to know him before unleashing the full effect. I have to say that when I see him hug someone who I know is like me, watching the awkwardness is hilarious. (Kind of like the montage of dads getting hit in the crotch by their kids on *America's Funniest Home Videos*. You never want it done to you, but it's a riot when it happens to someone else.)

On that first Roadshow tour, we were working on a documentary that was never actually completed and released. But because a film crew was shooting all the time, we would come up with these crazy things to do for the cameras. For example, in Seattle, a bunch of us went on a Segway tour to create content. (A Segway is a motorized, two-wheeled, self-balancing personal transport device that screams "Tourists!" to the locals.) Out on the street, Tim tried to convince a group of sightseers on foot that he was a tour guide. "Hey guys, I can show you around Seattle. Everyone follow me. I'll go slow. Just walk close so you can hear me." As charming and magnetic as Tim was, he wasn't able to convince them to go along. But, like always, he still won, because they all walked away smiling and laughing.

■

One day, I was watching one of the first edits from the documentary where the crew had interviewed Tim and his wife, Hilary. I heard them talking about Tim's cancer, something I knew nothing about at the time. In 2001, doctors had diagnosed him with a rare form of cancer and given him five years to live, at most. To remind you, this was 2013, at least seven years beyond their best medical prediction. I sat there listening, riveted to their powerful story, but in shock. They talked about how Tim had left his worship pastor position at Mariners Church in Irvine, California, and started meeting with homeless people and prostitutes under an overpass. Much like Rusty's transformation had impacted his life and ministry, following his diagnosis, Tim had gone through a similar change. Different catalysts, same outcome.

Tim explained, with his particular cancer, how he could live a long life or he could die tomorrow. The doctor's prognosis was unpredictable. I was struck and moved by seeing the emotion on Hilary's face. I also learned about the health emergencies and hospital stays they'd endured. In fact, he had to leave one tour due to health issues. Tim went on to explain how each morning after he wakes up, he realizes that God has given him another day. He takes a marker and makes an *X* on his wrist. Tim begins each day by reminding himself that his life has a God-ordained purpose. As he spoke, his wrist was stained from years of ink.

Tim begins each day by reminding himself that his life has a God-ordained purpose.

■

Everything was looking up in this newfound friendship, and then I find out he has cancer. My initial response to hearing this news was to separate myself from Tim. I suddenly felt like I had to prepare for his death. My guard went right back up, and I reminded myself, *I made a new best friend and now he's going to die. I'm going to lose him too. Of course he has cancer. The other shoe is about to drop on the one new friend I needed most. That's why it's better to not get close to anyone.*

Because of dealing with my dad dying of cancer, I wanted to pretend like Tim didn't have the disease. Losing someone else was not something I could go through again. But beyond the fear, deep down in my heart, I didn't want to keep Tim at a distance, so I opted instead for denial. My toxic thinking driven by my past grief kicked back in. Immediately, the accusation hit me that everything, everyone I touch gets ruined.

I know how awful this confession sounds. It's hard to admit, but in my continued effort to be transparent, that's where my attitude was at the time. My first real test dealing with tragedy in a couple years and I was failing miserably. While I didn't go back to the flower chair, for a little while, I went right back to the mindset.

But along with all this new information, I was suddenly given a very different perspective of Tim Timmons. His contagious joy became much more perplexing for me. He was the first person I had met who 100 percent understood what it was like to suffer from a chronic illness that never goes away and could take your life anytime. Every single day, Tim had to live with cancer, just like Sam had to live with diabetes. That realization created a common bond between Tim and me. And then, later, with Sam.

Here was yet another major connection for me: My response to Sam's diagnosis and 24-7 care was to go sit in the flower chair and drown in self-pity, while Tim had been told he was going to die and made the conscious choice to press on and be a conduit for joy. This challenge, as well as inspiration, reminded me of Tim's very first words: "Hey, I've been told I'm supposed to be your new best friend." Just like he predicted, we did become best friends. Tim's place in my life became another part of God's plan to bring about my transformation to the man I am today. There are certain people He doesn't just place in your life but seems to throw at you, as if to say, "I'm going to work through this person to help you, to accelerate you to transform into My image."

■

Shannon once told me, "Charlie [our middle son] is what you were like until 2004." She's right. Charlie reminds me every day of the better side of me. But after becoming friends with Tim while Charlie was still young, Tim was a reminder of "the old Bart," the epitome of joy. I clung to the fact that he was so positive, even with the cancer.

One day, I finally found the courage to tell Tim everything I had been feeling, with my ultimate confession being "Honestly, I really wish I hadn't found out about your cancer." Because Tim is Tim, he wouldn't allow me to get very far away. To this day, he will lean in and say, "You're not getting rid of me."

Shannon

On their first tour together, Bart and Tim connected quickly. Once Sam was also out with his dad, that opened the door for him and Tim to get to know each other as well. When Tim began to share about his cancer with Sam and told him everything he had gone through to learn how to manage the disease, their common bond was created. Tim was the first person in Sam's life who could understand *exactly* what he felt. Sam knew that he could never tell Tim, "You just don't get it."

I lost count of how many times Sam would ask, "Why me?! No one else I know has anything like this!" That's why, over time, Tim became a huge catalyst for Sam to begin to accept his diabetes, going from "no one understands" to "someone understands." As we said earlier, for someone suffering, empathy is so much better than sympathy.

After Tim and his family left California and moved to Nashville, we began going to the same church and then joined the same small group. We started doing life together. With so much connection and community, Tim became a mentor and discipler to Sam. He also started encouraging Sam in his music in a way no one else could.

Sam

The first time I met Tim was when Dad took me out to Grand Canyon University for my thirteenth birthday. I was immediately drawn to him, and then after their family moved to Nashville, we began to get close. Tim became one of my favorite people. One reason is because he is such a great listener. As I got to know him, I started talking to him about everything. Not just about diabetes but life. From chronic illness to relationships to faith, Tim was able to help me walk through anything. He has done more for me than he will ever realize. As a manly role model, outside of Dad, Tim is the most solid person in my life.

He also helped me through my last breakup with Chloe before our engagement. I will never forget him telling me, "I love your mom and dad so much, and I love you and Chloe. I love everyone in this situation the same." If I had a bad diabetic appointment, no one else understood like he did. The busyness of life may cause us to not see each other quite as much today, but nothing will ever change our relationship. One of my best memories is me, Dad, and Tim driving to Columbus, Ohio, to see John Mayer, an artist we all love whose music has been a common denominator for the three of us. As soon as the show was over, we got back in the car and headed home, driving through the night and talking about the show. Our passion for music is a strong bond.

Anytime I'm going through something and talk it over with him, Tim responds, "Sam, you woke up today." At first, I thought that was an odd response because he never explained what he meant. But he just kept saying it until I got it. And now, I say the same thing to people because I believe it's a super-powerful and simple truth. Randomly, Tim will text me, "You woke up today, so you have a second chance." That will stick with me for the rest of my life. That's the point of the *X* that Tim marks on his wrist every morning. He reminds himself and anyone who sees it that every day you wake up is a second chance.

Because Tim became such a close friend to both Sam and me, he naturally and supernaturally became an amazing bridge between us as father and son. Part of that was because of who Tim is and the other is his understanding of what life is like with a devastating illness. He is such a peacemaker who is able to see turmoil and feelings that Sam and I were too close to realize. Tim helped me finally hear and understand Sam's perspective of how I felt more to him like his doctor than his dad. He helped us see that our relationship had to become much more than that.

With Tim's help, Sam was finally able to tell me how he would watch me joke around and play with the other kids but then treat him like he was fragile and going to break. I didn't even realize I was doing that. Tim was the one to help me and Sam get out those feelings and understand those difficult dynamics. Like a good counselor, Tim was able to say things that I didn't feel I could say to Sam and help Sam tell me things he didn't think he could say to me. Because he has never seen any sort of disability or disease as a weakness or shortcoming, Tim was able to inspire Sam to realize he actually can change the world as a diabetic.

For our family, Tim was like a one-man rescue team that God sent into our house on fire, just in time to help me and my son get to safety and security.

IT IS WELL WITH (OUR) SOUL

Because Sam's story is such a major part of the plot of *I Can Only Imagine 2*, as well as in these pages, plus the catalyst for the song "Even If," naturally there is a lot of focus on him. That's why we want to dedicate this featured section to share about our other kids. For our complete story, getting a sense of who they are is just as important to us as who Sam is.

As a parent, you soon realize the double-edged sword that your children have some of the worst parts of you, but then they also have some of the best parts too. Today, we can look at all five of our kids and see strong characteristics in each of them that are different, but each one a part of us. All the time, Shannon or I will see one of our kids do something and say, "He's acting just like you," or "That's exactly what you would say." Going back to Psalm 139:14, we see how God has placed unique "fearfully and wonderfully made" qualities and traits in each of our children. Like all parents with their kids, you try to focus on those aspects and see past the days when they frustrate the heck out of you.

As a mom, when I (Shannon) get to witness my kids loving each other, those are the moments I can say, "Oh look, we've done something right." That bond between them was my main goal in parenting: for them to grow up wanting to spend time together for the rest of their lives. It's fine if they don't need me and Bart because they have each other.

GRACIE

November 4, 2004

Gracie has a special tenderness and kindness about her that makes her a natural caregiver. If she ever decided to become a nurse, she would be amazing. If something's wrong, you want her in your corner more than anyone. Here's a great example: In the summer of 2024, she decided to go back to Texas to stay with her grandparents (Shannon's parents). Gracie made the decision to get out of her comfort zone at home and go live in Greenville with them for a couple months. She would take their car and go pick up prescriptions or take Dad to get a haircut. Gracie would text a video and say, "I got Papa dancing in the kitchen," or "Look what I got Grandmama doing."

Those months ended up being the most beautiful time for the three of them as she took over their care. We know she will never forget those days and always cherish the memories they created together. The God-timing in her decision was that we had no idea Dad would be gone in November, only months away. That season she was with them created an even closer connection.

For me (Shannon), Gracie was the perfect person to be there. With our busy family, I couldn't have gone that summer to take care of my parents, so for Gracie to step up and step in to be an extension of me was such an amazing and totally selfless blessing.

CHARLIE
March 29, 2006

Charlie, our middle son, is the most like Bart. He's been a joy-filled, happy, positive kid from day one to today. As previously mentioned, he is Bart back before the whole world started falling apart and pulling at us. Charlie is super-extroverted, always ready to help, and a student of life. He constantly wants to learn and receive. Like Shannon, he is a sponge of information and remembers everything you say to him and anything he reads or watches and then wants to apply whatever he learns.

Charlie is an unbelievable drummer, but, like Sam, has a servant's heart and enjoys working on our tours over playing. Likely, he will end up playing drums for someone. Who knows? Maybe even his brother.

A favorite song of mine (Shannon) that Bart sang was for an album produced to go with the 2011 Max Lucado release of *The Story*. The song "It Must Be You" was about Moses and contained the phrase "'cause I'm tongue-tied." Hearing that lyric, I went to my Bible and looked up the passage in Exodus where Moses was still trying to convince God that He had chosen the wrong man. In Exodus 6:12, I read, "But Moses said to the LORD, 'If the Israelites will not listen to me, why would Pharaoh listen to me, since I speak with faltering lips?'" In *The Message*, Peterson says it this way: "And besides, I stutter." In verse 30, Moses reminds God one more time about his "stutter" (MSG).

After looking into this verse, I discovered that many theologians believe that Moses struggled with stuttering. In Exodus 7:2, God responded with His solution: "You are to say everything I command you, and your brother Aaron is to tell Pharaoh to let the Israelites go out of his country."

The reason why the song and discovering this detail about Moses was so important to me was because Charlie had started to struggle with stuttering. We could see how much this was bothering him and affecting his confidence. When I told him I had something to show him in the Bible, and after reading him these verses, I said, "God doesn't see this as a problem at all, Charlie. Moses stuttered and look how God used him. So if He calls you to do something and you need an Aaron, God will provide that person for you."

The beautiful result of our son hearing this story is that he never struggled again about his stuttering after that. He didn't worry or concern himself with it any longer. It just became a part of who he is. He didn't talk about the issue as much and simply accepted that he stutters. I think he felt like if Moses had the same issue, then he was in pretty good company. And, to this day, "It Must Be You" is one of Charlie's favorite songs.

SOPHIE

December 11, 2008

Sophie is our witty, funny personality with a definite artistic side to her. Over the years, like me (Bart) with Charlie, Shannon has said about Sophie, "She's the healthy me." She has a very tender heart like her mom. Today, with Shannon being in such a great place, the two of them are very similar. But, like all parents, the child that's the most like you is also the one who can "push your buttons" and cause you to bump heads.

Sophie is a true artist who's learned to sketch, watercolor, pencil, and oil paint, and even create pottery. She lets her emotions and feelings out on paper and canvas the way I (Bart) get mine out in songwriting. She also has my humor. Even when she was young, Sophie would communicate her feelings by writing them out. For example, when we can tell something is wrong and ask her about it, she may answer, "Nothing." But soon, she will show us a painting or drawing she did that will express whatever she was struggling with. One morning, I got a text from a pastor I know that said, "Hey, someone sent me this and I wanted you to see it." Sophie had posted a picture on her Instagram that she had drawn of the story the pastor had been teaching.

She is the more spunky, outgoing version of me (Shannon). During the Covid lockdown, as a family, we started an audio study on Israel. I was struggling a bit to stay with the content and wanted to find a way to engage the kids, so I suggested, "Why don't you all draw what you're hearing?" Sophie went to work and created a vision of art that could easily be a children's book on Israel. In fact, at the time of this writing, she is illustrating a kid's book. She is constantly creating art in some form from a deep well inside her heart.

One important Easter egg in the movie is the majority of the decor on the walls of "the Millard home" is Sophie's actual artwork.

MILES

March 21, 2011

Simply put, Miles, our youngest, is amazing. He is *all* boy. As we mentioned in an earlier chapter, Miles and Frank (Papa) were best friends. When he was little, he wanted "Papa shoes" and a "Papa shirt," which essentially made a toddler look like an old man.

Miles is a son who feels like a best friend, a ride-or-die. He will put everyone else in the family before himself. We do see a lot of Frank in him with a steady, soft-spoken, calm demeanor and temperament, no matter the circumstances. We have a lot of people tell us, "Man, Miles is the best kid on the planet," and my response (Bart) is always, "He gets that from Shannon." Kind with a steady confidence about him, he doesn't live and die by what his friends or anyone else thinks. If we ask any question of concern for him, the answer he'll commonly give is, "No, I'm good."

There's always something going on in our house, so Miles, being the youngest of five kids, doesn't have much opportunity to get bored. He's very in-the-moment. Yet, like me (Bart), he may slip off into a room by himself to do something alone. While, at this point, Miles has a phone, he doesn't have Instagram and doesn't seem to care, so he's not having to navigate the crazy peer pressure and comparison like so many kids his age deal with online.

Miles is the Millard family's house manager with the engineer brain from Shannon's family. His math skills are off the chart. He enjoys taking in data, which is why he loves baseball and memorizing player stats. The best thing we can say about Miles is he makes any room he's in better. While he doesn't like attention, his presence is always known. If we tell everyone in the family that on a certain day at a certain time, we all need to be ready to go somewhere, everyone else will forget. But that day, Miles will be reminding everyone of the exact details. He doesn't miss a thing.

Besides Chloe, Sam's best friend is his little brother Miles. Like our moms were, they've become sidekicks. Even in his twenties, Sam will call and say, "Hey, just letting you know I'm coming over to swim with Miles." How many twenty-three-year-olds want to hang out with their little brother, nine years their junior? But that says as much about Miles as it does about Sam.

THE SEVEN OF US

Frank's favorite song was the classic hymn "It Is Well with My Soul." He knew all our kids could sing, so for quite a while he had been asking us to have them sing and record the hymn. (One of the lines in "Even If" is "It is well with my soul," and in *I Can Only Imagine 2*, the hymn is sung by Movie Sam instead of "Because He Lives.")

After Frank's leukemia diagnosis in the fall of 2024, and after we were told he only had about a month to live, we knew we had to record the song for him. At the time, MercyMe was in the studio with Tedd T, the producer for the record, while Sam was also working on a version of the song to be in the movie. Tedd agreed to devote an evening to help us. We got all the kids together and mapped out what lines each one would sing. After working out the kids' parts, Sam took the intro, I (Bart) took a section toward the end, and then Shannon would sing the final lines, which was so appropriate for her dad to hear his daughter end his favorite hymn.

I had heard Gracie and Sophie sing before, and I knew they were both powerhouse vocalists. But I had never really heard Charlie sing before, except in the car or messing around in the house. Very early, he began to naturally hear and sing harmonies with his siblings, but we had never heard him sing a solo. We did know he actually sounds the most like me (Bart). Miles, as the youngest, was hesitant to sing by himself, but when we told him this song was for Papa, he was 100 percent on board. In fact, he sang the chorus.

After we finished the song, we sent it to Frank. When he was ready to listen, we gathered and watched him on FaceTime. When the song ended, he responded, "I knew you all could do this! I knew it!" Not long after the recording, we went back to Texas to see him. After a few days, for various reasons, we all had to get back home. Because he was doing better than the doctors predicted, we thought we had more time. Shannon's best friend, who is like a sister, was his nurse and gave constant updates. Just as were getting settled back at home, Frank took a turn, and she told us she felt like we needed to come back. Shannon needed to leave immediately, and Gracie was the only one who didn't have anything pressing, so they quickly packed a bag and drove back to Texas. Later that evening, the rest of us left and drove all night.

When I (Shannon) walked in, I said, "Daddy, I'm here. I made it." His countenance changed and his face lit up, as he said, "Praise God!" When I added, "And I've got Gracie with me too," Dad said, "Good morning!" At first, I thought that might be some confusion, but then Gracie explained that summer when she had stayed with them, she would usually take a nap at some point during the day. When she would get up and come back in the living room, Dad would always say, "Well, good morning," no matter what time it was. That was their own little inside joke, which explained that his response made perfect sense.

A while later, while everyone was out of the room for only a few minutes, Dad quietly slipped away. Gracie was the first person to go back in and realize she couldn't hear his labored breathing. When she came out to tell us, my friend and I went back in and saw he was gone. Bart and the other kids were still a couple hours away, still trying to get there.

Just like my friend had told me about Chris's death coinciding with Sam's birthday, I told Gracie how being the one to find her Papa was gone was such a hard moment at the time, yet, in the years to come, that would be a very special memory for her that no one else would have.

Dad listened to our family sing his favorite hymn on repeat until he passed. Today, that recording is an absolute treasure, a labor of love we would likely never have done for any other reason. We are so grateful he asked us to capture our voices together as a family, especially for such a timeless message of Christ's peace.

> For to me, living means living for Christ, and dying is even better. But if I live, I can do more fruitful work for Christ. So I really don't know which is better. I'm torn between two desires: I long to go and be with Christ, which would be far better for me. (Philippians 1:21–23 NLT)

Movie Moment

ON OUR WAY

Many iconic songs have been played as the final credits roll at the end of a major motion picture. So often, the song encompasses and enhances the emotions of the audience following the final scene. Here's the story of what is heard as the credits roll at the end of *I Can Only Imagine 2*.

As Sam began working with others to create new music, one of the popular avenues for songwriters the past several years has been to write "sync songs," meaning specific compositions targeted for use on TV or in film. Sam had heard that one of the popular TV singing competitions was looking for a certain type of song and, if chosen, was paying a flat fee.

Sam came to me one day and said, "Hey, I want you to hear this song that one of my cowriters and I wrote for TV. I think we have a real chance with this. We could make several hundred bucks. I want to see what you think." Of course, I couldn't wait to hear the song and listened intently. Right away, I let him know how much I loved it, but added, "Sam, this song is worth way more than a few hundred dollars. It's great!" Surprised, he asked, "Really? You think so?" I affirmed again, "Yes, absolutely; it's amazing."

At the time, we were in the middle of recording our 2021 album *inhale (exhale)*. One day, in a meeting with Jeff Moseley, the head of our label, I decided to play him Sam's song. My only goal was to show him how far my son had come with his songwriting. After Jeff heard it, he said, "Bart, this song is too good for Sam to sign it over to some TV show. Since he doesn't have a record deal himself, it should be on your record. That way, you get a great song and, as a writer, Sam has the opportunity to make much more money for a long time." Although I understood and agreed with everything he said, I responded, "Jeff, that's a weird place for me to be with my son. I don't know if I should ask him."

Knowing Jeff was absolutely right put me in a very tough position. I was trying to figure out how I could convince my son to let us record the song. I did feel it would be a great fit on our album. And Jeff was also right about the financial opportunity for Sam. But I knew how that could sound coming from his dad: "Hey, son, trust me, it's really good. Let *me* have your song." Then I could imagine Sam responding, "Wait, Dad, let me get this straight. You want me to give up several hundred dollars now to wait a whole year to make more?"

Jeff asked me if I would take Sam's track and record my vocal, just so we could see what it would sound like as a MercyMe song. Good idea. Before I talked to Sam, first, we needed to make sure it would work for us. The day I went in to sing, I was really sick. I managed to get the first verse and chorus out, but then couldn't sing the rest. My solution was to tell the engineer to keep Sam's vocal from his demo on the second verse. My plan was, if everyone, particularly Sam, agreed for us to do the song, then once I got better, I could go back and finish later.

Once Jeff, everyone at the label, and the band heard the song, they loved it. But when they heard the version with me *and* Sam, they all said the same thing, "Leave Sam on the song and make it a feature. People will love that it's you and your son and that he cowrote the song. Introduce him to the world." I promise you I had not had that thought. But I loved the fact that the idea came from our team and the band. Now, the final step was for me to go have my conversation with Sam.

I reminded him again that the song was too good to be signed away for a flat fee. Next, I told him the whole story about Jeff and what led to everyone wanting his vocal to be a feature. I also told Sam how this release would be introducing him not only as a singer and songwriter but also as an artist. I invited him to come out on our next tour to sing the duet with me each night. Everything made sense to Sam, so he asked his cowriter, who 100 percent agreed. In fact, his words were, "Dude! Let your Dad have it!"

The song is "On Our Way."

On the tour, Sam was the opener; then Crowder played next. During our set, Sam came back out for us to sing the song together, just like it is on the album. Even though it was never some strategic plan on anyone's part, this series of events launched Sam's career in Christian music. He's now managed by Brickell and signed with Jeff at our record label.

I completely respected his decision to be known as Sam Wesley (his middle name) to not make it obvious he was my son. He wanted to figure things out for himself, and I fully supported his desire.

Sam

When MercyMe decided to release "On Our Way" with my vocal as a feature, it led to people hearing who I am and what I do. I also got to see firsthand how Dad works, which helped me understand and find my own identity as a singer, songwriter, and artist. Dad does it his way and I do it mine, and that's good. After that, I felt like I could walk into a room and be seen as Sam and not just Bart's son or the kid with diabetes and the story behind "Even If." For all those reasons, "On Our Way" is very special to me. The song became such a defining moment for me as an artist, and also now as a man who God was allowing to find *my* way through His way.

Chapter 12

EVEN IF YOU DON'T

To tell the story of how the song "Even If" came to be written, the inspiration behind *I Can Only Imagine 2*, I have to rewind back to the story of our appointment in Nashville with Sam's new endocrinologist. On the drive there as the three of us were talking, Shannon told me about an encounter she had with someone we knew. After opening up and sharing everything we were dealing with in the difficult transition of doctors and the balancing act of our son's care, the person responded, "Well, we're just going to pray that Sam will be healed." Shannon then asked, "Why does that make me so angry?"

As I processed the person's statement, I blew past Shannon's question and cut straight to the heart of what we both felt and had become so frustrated and weary of hearing. Let's just say, I got *very* angry. Here was yet another time we had to deal with someone offering what they believed to be a well-meaning "spiritual" recommendation, but in reality, felt demeaning to us and, once again, came at the worst possible time. Over the years, it had become more and more difficult to push down the feelings those moments brought up and to try to avoid a confrontation by offering a short but kind response, especially when we were simply hoping for a listening ear or someone to just be present with no words. I couldn't bear hearing that, one more time, Shannon had poured her heart out only to get the obvious, easy Christian-ese "answer" thrown at her.

Immediately, I responded, "Oh, that's a novel concept! After fifteen years of struggling through this, let's try praying for our son! We never considered that as an option!" By the time we walked into the appointment with the new endocrinologist, a mix of anger, frustration, and hurt had welled up in me.

Because Shannon has already given the details of what happened after the doctor walked in, you know the rest of the story and how everything went horribly downhill from there. But the questioning and accusations of our care for Sam sent me over the edge. To this day, even through the deaths of family members, we both agree that was one of the worst mornings of our lives.

Shannon

After years of dealing with Sam's condition, when people would say, "Let's pray for his healing," that offer began to make my skin tingle with anger. My internal voice would scream, "Don't you think we've already done that thousands of times? What makes you think you're going to be the one who prays and Sam is suddenly healed? Is this about him or you?" I never blew up on anyone, but it's what I came to feel. I know people mean well, but being blunt, especially as Western-culture Christians, we can be both ignorant and arrogant when it comes to spiritual matters, especially something personal like prayer for others when we don't have enough context.

Because MercyMe was in the middle of recording our album *Lifer*, Tim and I had scheduled a songwriting session. The plan was for me to go to his house as soon as we finished with the doctor's appointment. In my fragile state of mind, I probably should have just gone home, but I figured talking things out with Tim would be good. Maybe, as had happened so many times, he could help me regain my perspective.

When I walked in, Tim asked, "Hey, Bart, what do you want to work on today?" His question prompted all my toxic emotions to reach a boiling-over point. Trying to fight back tears to no avail, I was at my absolute end. I started venting, saying things like, "Who does that doctor think she is, telling us we're killing our son?! What a horrible accusation after all we've been through for so many years!" Not even the flower chair would have helped me in that moment. Emotionally spent, as I went on, without thinking about who I was talking to, I made a terribly flippant remark: "It's chronic ... you wouldn't understand."

Tim didn't say a word. He didn't get angry or defensive or acknowledge my unintentional yet ignorant comment. True to his nature, he just gave me a kind, understanding smile. But I had no idea what to make of his next move. Tim walked over to his keyboard, sat down, and started playing random melodies. Right away, I felt like when you're giving an acceptance speech at an awards show and the orchestra starts playing to tell you to wrap it up, shut up, and get off the stage. Not yet finished with my fuming, I stopped a moment and stared at him. But Tim just kept on playing with his peaceful smile, occasionally looking at me, like he was the pianist at some swanky restaurant making pleasant eye contact with a patron. I thought, *He's not even listening to me! Doesn't he care about what I'm saying?!* I was so wrapped up in my own world that I hadn't yet realized I just told a man with incurable cancer that he wouldn't understand dealing with a chronic illness.

But I wasn't done. I wanted to keep verbally vomiting until I felt like I had gotten rid of all the emotional nausea. I started my rant back up from a different, deeply personal angle, "Man, I would give anything if people could see the real me, all the people that think I have it all together. The truth is, I just want to be like Shadrach, Meshach, and Abednego. Before they were sent into the furnace, they said, 'We know that God is able to deliver us, but even if He doesn't, we're still not going to bow down to your idol' [see Daniel 3:17–18]. If only I could be like them. But the truth is ... I'm not anywhere close. People think I am, but I'm so far from that."

Part of my venting was the desire to go to all the people who have told our family that we "just need to pray for Sam's healing" and ask them what happens, what do you do, how do you feel, where do you go next, when God *doesn't* heal your child? What great spiritual advice does everyone have then? When do we decide to pray that God will give us the strength to accept the circumstances and find joy in the suffering? To find Him *in* the fire? When do we come to the conclusion like Shadrach, Meshach, and Abednego that God may not ever make life "normal" again, but He may take us to a new place we never thought possible?

I ended by asking, "What do you say when you *aren't* saved from the fire?"

Tim never wavered from playing, never stopped to acknowledge anything I said. Finally, I snapped, "I'm going. We're not writing anything today." I stormed out, hearing the sound of his piano fade away as I closed the door and headed for my car.

Halfway home, I got a text with a voice memo attached. Seeing Tim's name, I thought, *Okay, this is going to be an apology.* But glancing over, I saw his brief message, "I tried to write that song five years ago."

I thought, *What does he mean by "that song"? We didn't even talk about a song.* Confused and curious, I found a good spot to pull over, tapped on the attached voice memo, and began hearing a keyboard intro. By the time Tim sang through the first verse and got to the chorus, I broke. My anger was relieved by the release of my tears. Soon after, Tim stopped and the recording ended, letting me know that was all he had.

I called Tim. "What is this?! We have to finish this song!"

Tim explained that he and Crystal Lewis (who also happens to be one of my Christian music heroes) had started the song five years before. Like Tim at the time, Crystal was going through hardships of her own. They were both relating to circumstances that felt impossible to bear and were trying to find the words to express their faith in the middle of grief, doubts, questions, and personal struggle. The partial song that Tim had played and sung on the recording was all they had written and never gone back to finish.

As I was purging, I had no idea Tim was actually in tune with every word I was saying. His playing was not ignoring me at all, but trying to find a jumping-in spot to write a song out of my feelings and questions. Tim told me he was thinking, *This is what we're here for, and you're saying a lot of powerful truths, so I need to find a song.* When I started to talk about the Daniel 3 passage, that's where he felt he should focus. Not long after I left, God reminded him of the song with Crystal from five years before. He quickly recorded what he remembered and texted it to me.

Once I got home, we continued the text thread, sending lyric ideas back and forth, which is a common way I work on songs with cowriters. Tim and I eventually got back together and finished "Even If" quickly. Once we dug back in, the rest of the song literally poured out. In fact, I wrote a lot more lines in the verses than we could fit with the melody and had to trim it back. As Tim and I were writing, he made a powerful confession: "I just want to get to the point with this cancer where I can say, 'It is truly well with my soul.' I can rest knowing God is in control." That's a tough place to arrive when you live daily with a threat like cancer. For him and Hilary, with everything they had gone through, he wanted to be able to say with complete freedom that he is okay with whatever God chooses to do or not do. Regardless, God is no less God.

Soon, I was back in the studio working on the *Lifer* album with Ben Glover, our producer on that record. After playing him my demo with Tim of "Even If," Ben and I worked through the entire song, and he helped me finalize all the thoughts I had. In that session, we recorded a final demo. Once the label and the band heard it, we fast-tracked the actual recording for the album. Being able to tell Tim that the song was going on our record was a fun moment. Our strange songwriting session had ultimately produced exactly what we had hoped. Actually, far more than we hoped.

■

For this album, we had all been adamant about releasing upbeat songs, wanting to avoid becoming known for another "power ballad." Our goal was to introduce this record with a fast, fun song on radio. For that reason, although we knew "Even If" had to be a single, it couldn't be the first. But that soon changed at an event in Phoenix where many of the Christian deejays from around the country were gathered and had invited us to play the album for them. I decided to hold "Even If" until last.

After playing the other nine songs, I announced, "That's the whole album, but there's one last song." After I shared the story of how it came to be written, there wasn't a dry eye in the house. Then, as they listened, by the time the final chorus hit, you could see everyone in the room resonate with the message. Witnessing the deejays' response, our record label decided

"Even If" had to be the first single. Afterward, they told me, "We have to swing for the fences on the first radio release, so this is it. This is the song!" Like Jesus said in Matthew 20:16, "So the last will be first."

Right out of the gate, the song charted faster than anything we ever released, including "Imagine." The number of streams went through the roof. In 2018, the song was nominated for a Grammy in the Best Contemporary Christian Music Performance and Song category. Backstage, I finally got to meet Crystal Lewis, who was partially responsible that this incredible song even saw the light of day. Because I never worked on the song with her, she and I had never met or talked. A fan more than a friend, I was so excited to meet her. Crystal explained how she and Tim had tried all day to complete the song, but just couldn't make anything work. When Tim called her to say we had finished and were recording it, she had trouble remembering it at first. For me, Crystal being part of the story made everything better.

■

As we began to play "Even If" every night, the best part was seeing the way so many people connected and resonated with the lyrics out of their own unique, difficult circumstances. The song seemed to help everyone feel like they weren't alone in their trials. For me, ticket sales or radio charts or record sales no longer mattered; I only wanted to be able to say, "This is the best I have and exactly what I want to say." I was so weary of feeling like I was showing people 10 percent of me every night and hiding the other 90 percent. My newfound understanding of God's grace and the freedom that had come from accepting that my identity is found only in Jesus gave me the desire to be real and transparent with nothing fake or contrived. I was ready to know that everything I say onstage is authentically who I am.

The first time Tim was with us when we performed "Even If," by the time the final chorus came, the whole crowd was standing with their hands in the air and tears in their eyes. Before the show started I'd told him, "You're not going to believe what you see when we play the song." I couldn't see him in the crowd, but I knew he was back by the soundboard. Afterward, he was blown away. It's always an incredible moment when you create something together and are able to witness how people respond after God lines everything up perfectly in the melody and the lyrics. That experience was another milestone moment for me and Tim.

At the point "Even If" came out and surprised us all, everyone in the band thought we were on borrowed time. We had been discussing the best time to ride off into the sunset. But then coupled with the synergy from the first movie, the message was clear that we weren't done yet. In so many ways, we felt like we were just getting started. We actually fell in love with music again and what we could create together. Even the parts of our career that had begun to feel like a burden we learned to enjoy again, but this time in an even deeper way. We were in a healthy place spiritually and felt like we truly had something new to share.

And how many times do you get a second chance—another opportunity to go around again?

■

The lyrics of "Even If" became my expression to say, "God, I know You're able to do anything. I know You can save or heal anyone in a moment with Your mighty hand. But *even if* You don't, my hope is in You alone." I felt like that line was opposite the majority of what is written in so much of Christian music. At least at the time we released the song, no one else was delivering a message like that. We need songs today like the psalms that say,

"When life doesn't go our way, God is still worthy of our trust, our hope, and our faith."

Lots of creative people sit down every day to try to write a hit. But it's the songs that are brutally honest, raw, and transparent that truly connect to what we all really need to hear, songs that help us get through the bad seasons in life, as well as celebrate the great times. Of course, it's way more fun to write a celebration song when life has been amazing. No one volunteers to be in the position to write an "Even If" out of actual experience.

Most Christian music is about God keeping us *out* of the fire. I wanted to echo Shadrach, Meshach, and Abednego's bold confession of faith to say, even if our God doesn't stop us from being thrown into the fire, He will see us through the fire. After many years and thousands of prayers, Sam hasn't been healed. In this story, we've told you all the circumstances where our family was not saved from the fire. After many years and thousands of prayers, Tim hasn't been healed either. His family was not saved from the fire. Yet the story became how God has seen us all *through* the fire. And today, He still does. "Even If" was born out of the storm of Shannon's and my ongoing struggles and questions regarding God amid faith and suffering. Out of those difficult years came the most honest and vulnerable lyrics I've ever written.

At the point I finally sat down to write "Imagine," the idea had been rolling around in my head and heart for nine years following Dad's death. When I was finally ready, the lyrics took about ten minutes. It felt as if I was a scribe taking down the words as fast as they were given to me. At the point that Tim showed me what he and Crystal had written of "Even If," I had been processing all those feelings for the past fourteen years of Sam's life. Once the song was finished, I realized I had been ready to speak that truth out loud for a long time. I just didn't know how. The reality of the birth of MercyMe's two biggest songs was that the actual writing only took minutes, while the life lived to accurately and honestly tell the story took many years. In the Bible, so many of the powerful stories were also years in the making, sometimes decades, sometimes even generations. We may be in a hurry, but God never is.

The toughest part of "Even If" for me was singing the lyrics in the bridge, the words that declare God's faithfulness and goodness when He has chosen not to heal, even though I believe He can. I understand why that's the part of the Christian life and faith so many people struggle to reconcile. That thought is very tough to confess. The looming question from a lost world becomes "So let me get this straight—you believe in a God who can save and heal, but He hasn't and doesn't appear like He will, and yet you still choose to follow and trust Him?"

In the Bible, so many of the powerful stories were also years in the making, sometimes decades, sometimes even generations. We may be in a hurry, but God never is.

Shannon and I finally came to the place of agreeing with Joshua's confession before God and the nation of Israel: "But as for me and my house, we will serve the LORD" (Joshua 24:15 NASB). Following Jesus is all about full and complete surrender to His will, which means dying to our own will. For us, that confession is deeply personal and emotional, which took me a very long time to be able to say for myself, much less sing to thousands. My fight in the flower chair was constantly about thinking, *God, You haven't been good. This is the worst time of my life when it should be the best.* But I had to accept the fact that, just like Tim's daily *X* on his wrist, I'm still here, Shannon and I are still married, and my kids are still here.

We are alive and together. This journey brought me to the point of being broken in the most beautiful way possible. In light of eternity and a home in Heaven, that is indeed *good*.

After "Even If," I decided that if I was to keep going in Christian music, then I wanted to talk openly about God's grace and our identity in Christ. That meant I would also need to continue being honest about the terrible moments of life too—when loved ones die tragically, your child gets a terrible diagnosis, or, like Tim, a doctor delivers the news that you only have five years left. I want the people in the crowd every night to know I am no different from them. I just happen to be able to sing and hold a microphone.

Shannon

"Even If" represents God's faithfulness to me, which has been both a gift and a blessing over the years, all while my humanity has pled with God to intervene. There's been such a wrestling with that reality, especially as I have read Jesus' miracles where He healed the blind, the crippled, and the diseased. As His daughter, that leads me to ask, "Why won't You answer *my* mother's-prayer to heal my son?" Then, I have to be honest with myself and ask, "Do I have enough faith to believe He would heal Sam?" When we suffer, so many questions are brought to the surface in our lives. There's no pretending or hiding when we are hurting so deeply. But then I always come back to Him and confess, "Thank You, Lord, that I still have my son."

"Even If" echoes my heart's cry for God, while also offering a prayer of thankfulness. Honestly, because I was angry for so long, I wasn't sure I would ever be able to arrive at that place of acceptance. I went through years of blaming myself, asking, "What did I do wrong? Did I somehow give Sam diabetes?" Our kids saw anger and sadness, nothing else. All our other emotions were gone. We had used them all. As the kids got older and we got healthier, we had to have some tough conversations and admit we didn't teach them how to feel and show all their emotions.

As Sam became a young man, my "Even If" connection with him was wrapped around my prayer that God would bring him together with a wife who would love him enough to partner with him in his care. Well, remember when I told you about the family vacation with Rusty's family and how Sam and Chloe became very interested in one another by the end of that week? Their relationship continued on through their teen years. Between 2013 and 2022, they broke up a few times, but always got back together, much like Bart and I did after knowing each other since childhood. On November 26, 2022, Sam and Chloe were married at the age of twenty.

Originally, they had planned on getting married on our anniversary, November 8, which was also my parents' anniversary, creating a legacy on that date. But then, soon after, Sam began to tour. That's when we told him and Chloe that Bart and I had rarely been together on our actual anniversary because most tours in the fall are still going on the eighth. So they moved to the weekend after Thanksgiving, which will never cause a conflict for a show date.

After enduring the flames of trauma after trauma, my struggle with believing that God could heal was a big mountain to climb. I had no problem believing He was capable, but I wasn't *living* like I believed it. The feelings and the fear can bring you to the place of asking, "So, God, if I truly let go, are You going to give me more pain?" Coming full circle back to Psalm 139, whatever the number of my days I have left, I will focus on what He desires for me to accomplish.

Sam

"Even If" came out of the season where we all felt so defeated. I was also dealing with my anger toward God, constantly asking, "Why do I have to go through this?" After that terrible follow-up with the endocrinologist, we got to the point where we'd had enough, because we didn't feel like there was ever a solution. Dad would always put on a brave face, so he came across as if he were stronger than everyone else. His go-to phrase was "We're going to get through this." But I remember hearing about him going to Tim's house after that appointment to write and how he had broken down, which I never knew of him doing before. I thought Dad was venting because he was upset with me. There had been other times like that when I might feel like he was mad at me because, at the end of the day, the diabetes was my issue. But later, I realized I had interpreted that wrong, and the misunderstanding was cleared up. Not until the past few years have I finally accepted and said, "This is *my* life. If I don't deal with it, I won't be here for very long. I have to grow up, let go of the anger, and take care of myself." While there's no cure on the horizon, the good news is we're doing great now.

Today, as a married man, my whole point of view has changed as I finally see all this through the lens of my parents. I have definitely gained an understanding of where they were coming from. My mom lived in fear of something happening to me during the night, which is why she couldn't sleep. Now, if I were in her shoes, I'd do the same thing. That's why there was more tension between me and Mom than Dad, especially when he was gone so much. I understand why she had so much trouble letting go, after being responsible for keeping me alive every day for so many years. Especially when the doctor told her that this didn't need to be her responsibility anymore, it would be so tough to back off and support from the sidelines. After the first few years of doing everything on my own, I finally understood their burden.

Especially as a teenager, I struggled with the contrast that there was not enough interaction with Dad but then too much with Mom. I knew we needed to somehow find a middle ground. The big shift came when Chloe entered the picture. She began to point out how our family dynamic wasn't healthy or balanced. Having an outside person come in who genuinely loves us and wants the best for everyone was so helpful. Chloe told me, "Your dad doesn't include himself in anything, and your mom is too involved. We're going to need to figure this out."

My first response to her was "Well, this is just how it is. Let's deal with it and accept it." That mindset permeated so many places to the point where there was not much relationship left. We were all just existing. But when Chloe ended up talking to everyone individually, we started realizing the truth and asking, "What have we been doing? This does need to change." My wife was the missing piece of the puzzle for our family. When we got married, Chloe and I had to tell Mom and Dad, "Look, this is our thing now. We're dealing with it together. I'm not saying this because I don't love you, but because I do. I don't want you to live the rest of your lives worrying about me and living in fear." That conversation was a big moment of release for our family.

As for my identity, for years, I lived my life trying to be something I'm not or trying to not be this person others assumed me to be. Since the moment I accepted who I was, I've been able to live in complete freedom. That feels so easy once you get it, but it can be a tough place to get to. If I hadn't gone through everything I have, I certainly wouldn't be who I am or where I am today. Once that weight was lifted, I became who God created me to be. I don't know why I was running and not proud of the family I was born into and the community I was blessed to be in. Once I accepted myself, all that fell into perspective. I don't see my life the same way I did before.

As cliché as this might sound, the greatest comfort we have in this life is our hope in Jesus. He is there and has been there the whole time. I wish I could have seen that when I felt alone, because I wasn't. It's so comforting to know He is with us and nothing in this life happens by accident.

All that I've gone through has only made me stronger.

And I wouldn't change that for the world.

Today, I'm grateful that, although Sam will always deal with diabetes unless there is a cure, it's not holding him back from pursuing God's call on his life and his own dreams. In fact, that's actually a big part of what motivates him. As his dad, I'm excited to step back, cheer him on, and watch him thrive.

■

When I was a kid, because Dad was at work until at least 5:00 p.m., I never had a ride home from school. I constantly bummed lifts from other people.

I didn't want them to drive me home because I was embarrassed for anyone to see my house. And I certainly didn't want anyone to come in because our place was always a wreck with three guys living there. Mammaw Millard lived in a rough part of town, so I didn't want to be dropped off there either. For those reasons, I would ask everyone to take me to my church, a place everyone knew. After Dad got off or Mammaw was out, one of them would eventually come pick me up there.

I would go into the church, sit in the quiet sanctuary, and sing because I loved how my voice echoed in there. Many afternoons, I would sit at the church piano, try to pick out songs with four fingers, and sing. One day, my pastor Dr. Summerall, who's also one of my heroes, was watching me through the little window in a side door. When I realized he was standing there, I was so embarrassed and stopped singing. He walked in, came over to me, and said, "Bart, if you can figure out a way to peel open your chest and let people see your heart, they'll follow you anywhere."

Ever since that moment, I have held Dr. Summerall's words close. "Even If" was definitely a moment where I peeled open my chest and allowed my heart to be seen. I showed the world a part of me I never had before. My pastor was right. The more we are willing to be transparent, the more others are willing to listen. Most people see through inauthenticity and can sense if we're real or not. It's the old saying "People don't care how much you know until they know how much you care."

I love that our two most well-known songs echo a phrase found in Matthew, Luke, and Acts: "Lord of Heaven and earth."

"Imagine" is about Heaven—our hope in Jesus that we will one day stand in His presence and see His face.

"Even If" is about earth—our hope in Jesus that we can hold on to through the fires and suffering in this life, until that day.

Conclusion

WE BELIEVE AND WE KNOW

The story told in the *I Can Only Imagine 2* movie, as well as this book, is not at all the same for me as the first film. I love that ending, but the memories of where I had been and where we were going are painful. While there have been extremely difficult parts to this story, I love how, as a dad to my son, we have worked everything out, just like my relationship with my father was ultimately worked out through reconciliation and resolve. Because of the Gospel we are able to tell the story that where we are now is much different and much better than where we once were. God's goodness ultimately changed three generations. A very different sort of happy ending—the kind God writes.

Once I finally came to agree with Paul's truth written in Romans 8:1, "So now there is no condemnation for those who belong to Christ Jesus"

(NLT), my renewed relationship changed the way I approach life and the way I approach being a husband, a dad, an artist, and a man. The acceptance of God's truth and grace allowed me to press on, have a short memory about others' choices, and live the life He has called me to live.

In the story of me venting to Tim, I asked the question "What happens, what do you do, how do you feel, where do you go next, when God *doesn't* heal?" What does that mean to your belief, to your walk with God? Where do you land? Do you walk away? Or do you stay and continue to follow? John 6:66–69 gives us a glimpse into this very human dilemma during Jesus' ministry.

> At this point many of his disciples turned away and deserted him. Then Jesus turned to the Twelve and asked, "Are you also going to leave?"
>
> Simon Peter replied, "Lord, to whom would we go? You have the words that give eternal life. We believe, and we know you are the Holy One of God." (NLT)

Through it all, Shannon and I arrived at the same destination as Peter. "Lord, to whom would we go? We believe, and we know you are the Holy One of God." We have come to trust He is good in ways we are not even certain of yet. In this world where everything changes so much and so fast, every day we can hold on to an ancient truth that's always there, remains the same, and never changes—the truth that has become the foundation on which everything my family and our band stand on: No matter how bad things get or how challenging the circumstances, God's goodness is consistent, available, and ever-present.

We can come to the place of confessing He is
my hope,
my better day coming,
the One who strengthens me to persevere,
the One who holds me,
the One who keeps me from giving up.

Even when I'm holding on to life by a thread, He's the thread.
The reason I keep fighting.
The grace poured out when I have nothing left.
He's never given up on me.
And He will never give up on you.
Our prayer is you too will one day say ...
"God, even if You don't ... I'll still put my hope in You."

NOTES

CHAPTER 4

1. Branden Harvey, "39 Most Inspiring Bono Quotes About Making a Difference," Good Good Good, May 9, 2022, www.goodgoodgood.co/articles/bono-quotes.

CHAPTER 5

1. Mayo Clinic Staff, "Reactive Arthritis," Mayo Clinic, January 25, 2022, www.mayoclinic.org/diseases-conditions/reactive-arthritis/symptoms-causes/syc-20354838#.

CHAPTER 7

1. "Diabetes & DKA (Ketoacidosis)," American Diabetes Association, accessed September 22, 2025, https://diabetes.org/about-diabetes/complications/ketoacidosis-dka/dka-ketoacidosis-ketones.

Free Companion Bible Study

This six-session Bible study, inspired by *Even If*, weaves together excerpts from the book along with Scripture-based lessons on faith and perseverance. Designed for small groups or personal study, each session invites thoughtful reflection and practical application to help you grow your faith in Christ.

DOWNLOAD YOUR COPY

DAVID C COOK

transforming lives together

JOIN US. SPREAD THE GOSPEL. CHANGE THE WORLD.

We believe in equipping the local church with Christ-centered resources that empower believers, even in the most challenging places on earth.

We trust that God is *always* at work, in the power of Jesus and the presence of the Holy Spirit, inviting people into relationship with Him.

We are committed to spreading the gospel throughout the world—across villages, cities, and nations. We trust that the Word of God will transform lives and communities by bringing light to the darkness.

As a global ministry with a 150-year legacy, David C Cook is dedicated to this mission. Each time you purchase a resource or donate, you're supporting a ministry—helping spread the gospel, disciple believers, and raise up leaders in some of the world's most underserved regions.

Your support fuels this mission.
Your partnership sends the gospel where it's needed most.

Discover more. Be the difference.
Visit DavidCCook.org/Donate